RUN
FOR MY
LIFE

JOSEPH P. O'DONNELL
AS TOLD BY DANIEL KOLMANN

outskirts
press

Dedication

This book is dedicated to the three most important women in my life:

My mother, Erna "Netty" Kolmann who endured the incredible horrors of Nazi antisemitism during World War II and the repressive regime of Communism in the post-war era of Czechoslovakia. Despite the incredible pain of losing members of her family to these ruthless oppressors, she remained strong and defiant, while at the same time, never losing the ability to be kind and loving. The strength of her character and her bravery were an inspiration to me as a young child and continues to this day. I will always remember her as a loving mother and a true hero. I am also eternally grateful for her support and encouragement for me to defect from Russian-occupied Czechoslovakia and seek freedom and happiness in the United States.

My half-sister, Ana, who, as a young girl in Czechoslovakia, witnessed the horrific brutality of the

Nazi policy to exterminate the Jews. Fortunately, she survived, emigrated to Israel after World War II, and eventually immigrated to the United States where she became a naturalized citizen. I will always be thankful for her love, advice and support during the period of my escape and arrival in the United States.

My wife, Karina, who has been at my side for more than thirty-seven years and has brought much happiness to my life. I am deeply indebted to her for her love, undying support and encouragement for me to write this book.

Daniel Kolmann

To Ronney:

My wife, my outstanding editor and always my best friend.

Joseph P. O'Donnell

Table of Contents

Chapter One

I WAS BORN in St. Martin, Czechoslovakia on May 30, 1948—three years after the end of World War II.

The war had taken a heavy toll on Czechoslovakia during its occupation by the Germans from 1938-1945. The population had been forced to devote all of its efforts to the Nazi war machine. By 1939 Czechoslovakia had become a major center for military production for Germany—manufacturing aircraft, tanks, artillery and other armaments. (1, 2)

Overall, Czechoslovakia was devastated by World War II. Nearly one million people out of a pre-war population of 15 million had been killed. (2, 3) Furthermore, despite Czechoslovakia's value in providing forced labor, the country had been victimized by Germany's campaign of "ethnic cleansing." Altogether, 265,000 Jews were murdered by the Nazis by the end of the war. (2, 3)

For my mother, Erna "Netty" Kolmann, my birth was a true blessing—another son to take the place of the two sons she had lost in the war. Her sons had not, however, been casualties of wartime conflict. Instead, as Jews, they and my mother's first husband were arrested by the Gestapo, taken to a concentration camp and never seen again.

Eventually, during the World War II years of German occupation of Czechoslovakia, news spread in Bratislava—the city where my family lived—that the Nazis were not only targeting the Jewish men and boys, but had also begun to arrest the Jewish women and girls. Fearing for the life of Ana, her ten-year-old daughter, my mother stashed a supply of food into a large sack and left her home with Ana in the darkness of night. They hid in a forest area outside of Bratislava for several days. When their food supply had been exhausted to all but a few sugar cubes, they began a long walk on the forest's edge to seek refuge from the Nazi soldiers.

They came upon a farmhouse owned by a Christian couple that took sympathy upon their plight. This wonderfully kind and brave family risked their own safety to hide my mother and Ana under piles of hay in the loft of their barn. When the Gestapo arrived to search the farm, as they did almost routinely, to look for Jews that had escaped from the cities, the soldiers placed bayonets on the ends of their long rifles. Then they reached upward to poke through the hay hoping to find hidden Jews.

Fortunately for my mother and Ana, they were never discovered.

My half-sister, Ana—sixteen years old when I was born—and my mother survived this ordeal and remained in Bratislava after the Germans were driven out of Czechoslovakia and the Russian occupation and influence began.

My mother had married my father, Josef Kolmann, who was also Jewish and, years earlier, had been taken to Poland by the Germans. But he was among the few to escape from Terezin—another of many concentration camps—by boldly cutting through a wire fence. In the process, he lost a part of one of his fingers, leaving a scar that served as a reminder of the desperation and bravery required to successfully complete such an escape.

My mother had two brothers—my uncles—who quickly recognized the threat of the impending Russian takeover of Czechoslovakia at the end of World War II. With my mother's approval, they took Ana to Israel shortly after I was born to avoid living under the repressive single-party rule of the Communist Party within Czechoslovakia—a totalitarian regime that had seized control with full support of the Russian government.

The Communist Party of Czechoslovakia—with Russian backing—maintained this undisputed control of Czechoslovakia for more than four decades. (4)

In the years after World War II, my father had become a highly skilled soft-electrical engineer with additional knowledge pertaining to the design of computers. Thus, he possessed expertise in a field of great importance to the Russians: computer technology that was a critical component in the goal of expanding their dominance in tank warfare.

My mother, a strong and highly intelligent woman, had her own level of expertise in the area of ordering and distributing essential food products and household materials. This experience resulted in her appointment as the primary purchasing agent in Bratislava. In this coveted position she developed close connections to major members of the Russian-controlled Slovakian government.

This was a period of great shortages of food and household supplies for the population at large. Everyday essentials such as milk, bread, eggs, and bananas were often not available.

Shelves in stores were often bare.

Food lines developed.

At times, more than one hundred people could be seen standing in line for more than an hour just to get a loaf of bread.

My mother, however, never forgot the kindness and bravery of the Christian family that offered Ana and her safe refuge from the Nazis. Because of the food shortages that were part of daily life, she often arranged for deliveries of food right to their farmhouse.

In addition, my mother made sure that the local government officials never endured the hardships of food shortages. Similarly, food and other essential items—paper products and even sundries—were delivered to their homes. These deliveries were never acknowledged in writing. No paper trails existed. Such transactions were handled with merely a wink or a nod. As a result, my mother accumulated a wealth of "owed" favors that helped her to achieve a certain level of power over these officials that not only served our family very well while I was still a young boy, but proved to be a valuable resource later in her life.

My mother always impressed me by the highly efficient and quiet manner in which she carried out the functions of her position. Then she used its inherent power to her full advantage in order to help her family as well as others in need. By remembering those who had helped her in the past, she taught me the importance of gratitude and kindness. By cleverly gaining control over the corrupt Communist bureaucrats in our city, she demonstrated her quick-witted mind and un-yielding resolve to never surrender to these oppressors.

The strength of my mother's character remains as the most powerful influence on my life.

Chapter Two

THE RUSSIAN OCCUPATION and communist control of Czechoslovakia marked a continuation of the severe antisemitism that began with the Nazis in World War II. Since my family and many of our friends were Jewish, the impact of this prejudice was felt on a near daily basis.

Some synagogues were destroyed by fires—most of which were of mysterious origin.

Czechs were not allowed to assemble in large numbers anywhere in our city.

No more than six people were permitted at a religious service.

KGB, the Soviet Security Guards, stood outside of temples and churches to intimidate members and verify that they adhered to these rules. In order to attend Friday night Shabbat services, some daring members of our temple actually sneaked in through back doors to defy this assault on religious freedom. Stories circulated, however, from the capital city of Prague that, when the rule of "no more than six" was violated, the KGB burned down the temple or church. Fortunately, at our temple none of our "daring" members were ever detected.

Similarly, when I reached my eleventh birthday and began the process of preparing for my Bar Mitzvah, our Rabbi had to secretly come to our house to teach me the Torah. Since such teachings were prohibited by the Communists, he had to use a back entrance to elude the scrutiny of the Russians.

My Bar Mitzvah took place in our home on a Friday night just after my thirteenth birthday. It was attended by a total of eight people, a few who entered through our front door and the others that sneaked in through the back entrance. I have often considered it to be the smallest and most clandestine Bar Mitzvah that ever took place in Czechoslovakia. But, my mother, in her own creative way, prepared a delicious meal that included challah, chopped chicken liver, potato pancakes, matzo ball soup, breaded chicken cutlets, broiled chicken, boiled potatoes, and three special desserts—cookie pudding, apple strudel and choco-late babka.

It was a very special event—one that I will never forget.

The wave of antisemitism that permeated life in

Czechoslovakia still caused my father to be viewed with disdain and suspicion by the ruling class. There were days when the KGB spied on our house from another property located diagonally across from ours.

As a young boy, I was totally unaware of this intrusion.

My father, however, picked up on several obvious clues of this surveillance and took subtle but decisive measures to prevent it. He built a fence around our house that, by all appearances, seemed to merely be a physical enhancement to separate the property from neighboring homes. But, by taking full advantage of his engineering expertise, he electrified the fence with a warning signal—a bell in the kitchen—to alert us anytime someone crossed through the fence and walked toward our house.

Since this was the era of the "Cold War" between Russia and the United States, the threat of nuclear bombs was a great concern to the population of Czechoslovakia. My father, tapping into his knowledge of civil engineering, designed and built a concrete bunker seven feet underground in the rear of our property.

This bunker had ten steps leading underground to a metal door that opened up to a room that could accommodate six people. The concrete roof extended above ground for approximately one foot.

In addition, my father's sharp mind and engineering background helped our family to get by those periods of extreme shortages of certain foodstuffs. He built a "fake wall" within our house where my mother could store non-perishable items such as flour, sugar, salt, canned foods, and, of critical importance, currency.

Cash was an essential commodity in Communist-occupied Czechoslovakia where "greasing the hand" of certain officials, both Czech and Russian, was a way of life.

The Russian government also had strict rules pertaining to news and information from "The West" being received and disseminated within Czechoslovakia. Such news reports were often "scrambled" to further hinder their reception. If the owner of a house in our town was found to be receiving news reports via Radio Free Europe, he or she could be sentenced to ten years of hard labor in a Russian prison camp.

My father, however—once again utilizing his great technical mind—figured out how to "descramble" the interference so he and my mother could listen to Radio Free Europe on a regular basis without ever being detected.

Over a period of years, however, my father's "perks" from his position as an engineer and a technical asset to the Russians caused him to undergo many changes in his political philosophy. He began to fully recognize his value to Russia's ultimate goal of military dominance and the "protection" afforded him by his skill. He also began to believe in the Communist party and, by his close association with their leaders and ultimate acceptance of their rule over our country, he felt that his own power had actually become enhanced.

As a young boy, my only awareness of these changes was brought on by differences in his behavior. He demeanor became more serious and he began to speak to me in a very strict tone. We only interacted on those times when he tried to teach electronics to me. I was interested in sports, particularly soccer, on which he placed little or no value. In fact, despite my skill as a young soccer player, my father never came to one of my games. My mother, on the other hand, never missed a game—rain or shine,

My father also began to socialize with his fellow communists and began to view them as his closest friends. He would even invite them to come to our home. On these occasions my mother had to cook elaborate meals and entertain them. Despite disliking them intently and everything they stood for, she did this to protect my father from any incriminations.

Unlike my father, my mother's friends were the

elite of the Bratislava community—doctors, lawyers and other professionals who the Communists allowed to pursue their careers because they were so vital to maintaining the money stream of the local economy.

My mother, always brave and defiant, often hosted elaborate dinner parties for these friends, despite the fact that such gatherings were forbidden. In retrospect, I believe she relied on the "protection" afforded by her position as the primary purchasing agent in Bratislava. None of the officials she bribed with goods and merchandise wanted to risk falling out of her favor. My father, on the other hand, would conveniently excuse himself from attending these dinners with my mother's friends, citing an important "meeting" related to his job.

As I grew older and entered middle school, the theme of everything in Bratislava was "Mother Russia." The boys were required to wear white shirts, blue pants and a red tie every day. We were forced to learn to speak Russian and were taught that Russia had saved us from the Nazis.

We were also shown videos and pictures of American slums—bums and homeless people on Canal Street in Manhattan—all with the singular purpose to verify that capitalism was a failure.

My class consisted of twenty-two children that

stayed in one room for the entire day while the teachers of different subjects rotated from room to room.

One of our teachers, Mrs. Eva Podmonkova, was an attractive woman of medium height. Even now, more than fifty years later, her image is as fresh in my mind as if I had seen her yesterday.

My memory of her, however, is not based on her outward appearance.

Rather, her antisemitic comments were so blatant, it seemed that she couldn't care less about how they could be so upsetting to a young person.

One day, as I inadvertently opened one of my books from left to right, she walked past and said with a sneer, "Are you expecting to read Hebrew?"

I was twelve years old and very embarrassed to have been singled out in this way in front of my classmates.

When I got home and told my mother, she was furious.

But there was nothing she could do.

Such insensitive, discriminatory remarks were part of everyday life in Russian-controlled Czechoslovakia.

I quietly vowed to get even.

During the cold winter months, when Mrs. Podmonkova entered our room, she would immediately sit on top of the radiator lid to warm up. I took notice of this pattern and hatched a dastardly plan to carry out my revenge.

One day before leaving school, I stole some phosphorous powder from our physics lab, stored it in a small plastic bag and shoved it into my pants pocket.

Then I hid the bag in my bedroom and waited for just the right opportunity.

Later in the week, on a typical winter day in Czechoslovakia—bitterly cold with winds that chilled right to the bone—I carried out my plan.

In between subject classes, while no teacher was present in our classroom but knowing that Mrs. Podmonkova would soon arrive, I walked over to the radiator.

I looked around the classroom.

My classmates were busy with chatter and the usual fooling around.

No one was watching me.

I lifted the covering lid, and sprinkled the phosphorus powder directly onto the hot radiator.

Then I quickly walked away and sat down in my seat.

Several minutes later, Mrs. Podmonkova entered the classroom, took off her coat and, while briskly rubbing her hands together, immediately walked over and sat down on the radiator cover while she took attendance.

I could feel my heartbeat increasing with anticipation.

Perhaps pounding is a better adjective.

Suddenly a distinct "poofing" sound was heard.

Every kid in the class looked over to see what had happened.

Flames erupted from underneath the radiator cover.

Mrs. Podmonkova let out a terrifying scream as she jumped up from her sitting position.

She became frantic when she saw that her skirt was on fire.

She ran toward the door screaming for help.

A pungent, garlic-type odor filled the classroom.

We sat in our seats stunned by the scene that had unfolded in front of us.

I said nothing.

She was rushed to the hospital for treatment of severe burns on her skin.

The KGB showed up, closed the school for the day, and locked the doors so no one could leave. They immediately conducted an investigation—interrogating every student in the class and, over the course of a few days, every parent.

These interrogation efforts, however, were unproductive. No one was ever determined to be the culprit that placed the phosphorus on the radiator.

Interestingly, my parents never questioned me about this incident.

I think they knew I was the prankster, but all of us seemed satisfied to just let it fade away.

Mrs. Podmonkova, however, was not of the same mindset. Over time, she continued to press the school authorities for justice. She wanted someone arrested and punished.

I disliked her more than ever.

I found out that she lived around the block from our house.

One day, as I casually walked by her house, I noticed that she had a cherry tree in her backyard.

I looked around.

No one in sight.

I jumped over the fence, picked all the cherries, cradled them in the rolled-up bottom of my shirt, and brought them home to my mother.

My mother was not happy but did not punish me. More than any other person I knew, she had endured the most vicious effects of antisemitism and understood the need to strike back at those that embraced it.

She rinsed off the cherries and placed them in a bowl.

Then we sat down at the kitchen table and ate them.

This was a quiet act of defiance that I loved sharing with my mother.

Several months went by uneventfully. Then one day,

Mrs. Podmonkova came to our house and stood at our front door to speak to my mother.

"I know your son is responsible for putting that chemical on the radiator," she said. "But I have no way to prove it."

My mother remained calm while speaking in a direct and emphatic manner. "You have no basis for that accusation and there is no reason for you to mistreat my son or speak to him in a derogatory manner in school. If you do, I will report you to the government authorities and insist on your dismissal."

Mrs. Podmonkova walked away without saying a word.

My mother never discussed this matter with me again.

Chapter Three

DURING MY MIDDLE school years, I became very active in sports. Running was my specialty.

I could run like the wind.

I was always the fastest runner—not only in my class but in the entire middle school. My speed helped me to excel in soccer, and I was soon recognized as one of the best players in the school.

One day two men from the Slovakian Sports Authority came to our house. They were accompanied by two members of the KGB that stood quietly behind them.

"Your son has been observed to be a good athlete," one of the men said.

"Yes," my mother replied. "We are very proud of him."

But as the men continued talking, my mother's eyes widened and her mouth dropped open.

She looked frightened.

The lead official from the Slovakian Sports Authority

began to speak in a very harsh tone.

"Your son is going to be trained as a soccer player in a sports camp. He will be living in a dormitory with other athletes. You will be able to see him once a week," he said.

"No...no!" she screamed. "You can't take him!"

She stood in front of me, in a desperate attempt to use her arms to shield me from their grasp.

"I lost two sons in the War," she cried. "Please ... please don't take him from me!"

I cowered behind her, not knowing what to do.

One of the KGB officers took control of the encounter and stepped forward, almost face-to-face with her.

"You no longer own him; the State owns him!" he said. "The State has the right to remove him from this house!"

My mother pushed him away and continued to resist.

"You dirty Communist! Don't you have any feelings for me? He's my only son!"

The two KGB officers looked at each other and exchanged a nod.

Then one of them forcibly shoved my mother aside. She fell to the floor.

The two men from the Slovakian Sports Authority were stunned but did nothing.

The other KGB officer grabbed my arm and began pulling me toward the door.

I twisted my body away and tried to kick him in his legs. But the lead officer joined him to grab me from behind, put his arms around my chest and totally restrained my upper body while the second officer controlled both of my legs.

My mother continued to scream and cry—wailing like a wounded beast—as the two KGB officers carried me away to their car.

Her sounds are still with me today—painfully etched into my memory as vividly as the day they occurred.

In my later years, as I think back to that day, I understand the devastation that she must have endured at that moment. She had already lost two sons during the Holocaust. Now, her only remaining son had been taken away from her by coercive force.

At the sports camp I and the rest of the young athletes were assigned rooms in the dormitory. I missed my family, but quickly realized that I had no choice in this matter. I knew I had to adjust to my new life.

I also knew that the armed guards, providing security for the camp's perimeter, were there to make sure that none of us attempted to leave. But the presence of the guards and their guns created an eerie sense of tension that pervaded the entire camp grounds. I stayed away from them and never engaged in conversation.

Our daily schedule was quite rigorous: 7:30 am to 1:30 pm—school; 1:30 pm to 6:30 pm—soccer.

A man named Dr. Meyer was in charge of the sports program. He had a PhD in physical education and established the training programs for the athletes. He also had control over the home visitation schedule. This rule stated that the athletes could go home every seventh day if they maintained a record of good behavior.

But Dr. Meyer was another anti-Semite. He knew that I was Jewish and found reasons to put me on probation so that I was only allowed to go home once every thirty days—the minimum mandatory home visitation requirement.

Despite the restrictions on my home visits, the intense training and coaching in the sports camp caused my proficiency in soccer to flourish. I rose to the top echelon of the boys' soccer players and became the leading scorer. As such I was a member of the camp's first team that played in junior competitions throughout Czechoslovakia.

By age fourteen, a fluke encounter caused me to branch out to other sports besides soccer.

The tennis courts were located nearby the soccer fields. One day, on my way back to the boys' dormitories, I stopped to watch a guy warming up for a tennis game.

He noticed me and asked, "You want to hit some balls?"

"Sure," I said.

He handed a spare racquet to me and we started volleying back and forth.

A tennis coach sat on a nearby bench and began watching us.

Within a short time, I was maintaining a steady back and forth volley with this experienced player. I was also able to run and get almost every ball that he hit to either side of me, including those that were hit short or over my head. I had no idea of the rules of tennis, but was sure that hitting the ball back over the net was fundamental to winning a point.

The tennis coach got up from his seat on the bench and walked over. "Excuse me, son. I haven't seen you before on the tennis courts. What's your name?"

"Daniel Kolmann."

"Who's your coach, Daniel?"

"I don't have a tennis coach. I'm a soccer player. This is the first time I've ever been on a tennis court."

He smiled.

"Do you know that the man you were hitting balls with is one of the top tennis players in the camp?"

I looked over at the guy who had been volleying with me.

"No, I never saw him before today."

He put his hand on my shoulder.

"I'll be speaking to Dr. Meyer," he said. "From now on, you're going to be a tennis player."

During the next two years, I took lessons and trained hard as a tennis player. The game seemed to come naturally to me, but I practiced with a ferocious mindset in order to improve. A cement wall to the side of the tennis courts was used to practice volleying. Whenever I had a free minute, I grabbed my racquet, went over to this wall and practiced my ground strokes. In short time, my forehand and backhand shots became very strong.

The more they developed, the more I wanted to practice.

My speed also helped me and I used it to develop good foot work that was necessary to become proficient in the sport. Soon I began to beat the top junior players in the camp and won several tournaments— both singles and doubles events.

My mother missed seeing me at home, but began to appreciate that the intensive sports training was having a positive effect on my physique and athletic prowess.

I had become bigger, stronger and faster. My ground

strokes had become powerful; my serves were like miniature rockets.

My mother was very proud of my accomplishments and sent some of the newspaper articles about my tennis victories to Ana, my half-sister in Israel.

But the Communist government read every letter that was mailed. Their "screeners" would open the letters, read the content, and then re-seal and mail the letter only if the content was innocuous. Any correspondence that showed our government or the Russians in an unfavorable light was destroyed.

At times, my father had to employ a somewhat clandestine approach to send mail to Ana. He would somehow get a letter to a friend in Romania and from there it was mailed to Tel Aviv.

By 1962 my mother had not seen Ana for nearly fourteen years. Ana wanted to visit us in Prague, but travelers from Israel were not allowed. Similarly, travel from Czechoslovakia to Israel was prohibited. My mother appealed to the local Board of Governors for a special permit to allow her to make a one-time visit to Israel.

At first her appeal was denied.

However, her appointment as the head purchasing agent in Bratislava had evolved into one of the most important positions in our city. The members of the

Board needed to remain on her good side in order to maintain the steady flow of high-quality food and sundry items she provided.

In addition, she had learned to resort to the customary manner of gaining favor with corrupt bureaucrats: she paid them off. Over time they had become accustomed to the extra money that greased their palms.

She made a second appeal to the Board to reconsider her request to make the trip to Israel. This appeal had a two-pronged approach:

1 She would provide any guarantee they required to ensure that she would return to Bratislava after one week.
2 If they denied the appeal, she would cut them off—no further "perks" for any of them.

After considerable discussion, my mother and the Board agreed to the following conditions: She had to sign a document by which ownership of our house would be turned over to the Board Members if she did not return. Furthermore, if she stayed in Israel longer than one week, my father would be imprisoned.

My mother was thrilled to reunite with Ana after so many years and to meet her husband, Oscar, and her son, Martin—my mother's first grandson. Ana had become quite successful in Israel as the owner of a jewelry business in Tel Aviv. She was also grateful that my mother and her uncles—my mother's brothers—had had the foresight to get her out of Czechoslovakia before the borders were slammed closed by the Russians.

As promised, my mother returned from her trip within a week and had become more determined than ever that I needed to meet Ana. Again, through her contact with the Slovakian-Communist elites, my mother arranged for us to obtain permission to travel to Warsaw, Poland—a city within the Soviet-bloc—where we met Ana.

This was an exciting experience for Ana and me, since it was our first meeting.

She was 31; I was 15.

We talked for hours about our respective lives: Ana's in Israel—a free country; mine in Czechoslovakia—a Communist country where the citizens were under the total control of the government. Although it was only our first meeting, we struck an immediate bond—one that would last for the rest of our lives.

She asked about the sports camp, my success as a tennis player, my plans for the future, and my thoughts about living under the control of such an oppressive government.

At one point during the afternoon, she leaned toward me.

"Moishe," she said. "When you have the opportunity, you must escape."

I was stunned by her words.

"You mean defect?" I asked.

"Yes."

"But we are guarded by the KGB. They have guns and powerful rifles. It would be dangerous."

"I know," she said. "But you must find a way."

I didn't respond.

She reached over and gently placed her hand on my cheek.

"My sweet little brother...you must understand. They will exhaust all of your talent while you are young. And when you are no longer a star, they will have no use for you. They may even decide to do away with you. Never forget...these are ruthless people."

For a fifteen-year-old, these words were difficult to process.

I sat quietly.

Ana reached into her purse and took out a pen and a small notepad. She began jotting down some information as she spoke.

"There is a Jewish organization...HIAS...they help Jews get out of Communist countries. Memorize these initials and then throw this paper away so it's never found in your possession. When you escape, somehow try to reach them. They will get you to the United States."

I was completely unnerved by her comments.

I stared at the paper for a few seconds. Then, without saying a word, I folded it and shoved it into my pants pocket.

Later that night I memorized the initials. Then I tore the note into a dozen little pieces and threw them into the trash.

The next day, my mother and I returned home.

On our train ride back to Prague, I didn't expect my mother to discuss Ana's advice. In fact, I had no idea that she had any knowledge of my conversation with Ana.

Having already lost two sons and her first husband to the Nazis, I assumed the topic was too emotional for her.

But I was wrong.

My mother had the strongest will of any person I ever knew. The incredible experiences of her life and the losses she endured—unbearable by most standards—had made her remarkably tough.

She was a fighter.

She learned from the pain in her past and kept moving forward with determination, never allowing negative experiences to defeat her.

She looked over to me.

"Ana was right," she said. "You have to find the right time and the right place to escape. If you don't, you'll have no future in our country."

She looked away and said nothing more.

But her words were powerful and resonated within me.

I paused for a few seconds.

"I know," I said.

Chapter Four

DURING THE REST of the train ride, I had time to think back to the terrible comments directed at me over the past few years at the sports camp. Even though I had become the #1 player on the Junior Tennis Team, I was frequently viewed primarily by my Jewish heritage more so than my proficiency as an athlete.

I was often the target of derisive antisemitic slurs.

At times when I walked over to the bench—sweating profusely after a highly competitive tennis match—the KGB guards would flash a condescending look toward me and say, "Smelly Jew."

Although such comments were highly offensive, I accepted the reality that I could not respond.

To retaliate meant severe disciplinary action, including weeks of confinement in the dormitory—even imprisonment.

Possibly worse.

But now, the thought of such comments intensified my desire to take action.

When I returned to the sports camp, I began to view everything—my training, my goals, my future—in an entirely different light.

I developed an inner burn, and it never went away.

Dr. Meyer only exacerbated my feelings by continuing to show his profound antisemitism. He always treated me in a most disrespectful manner and downplayed my rapid improvement in which I had become the best tennis player in the camp. At times I looked over at him while he watched one of my matches and assumed he was hoping I would lose. This feeling motivated me to play even harder.

My dislike for him became more intense with each passing day.

He became a symbol of the repressive regime that ruled my life.

On Dr. Meyer's orders, Dunlop Max Fly racquets—the newest technology in the game—were distributed to all the players on the Men's team except me. I was forced to play with an out-of-date Slovakian racquet of low quality that put me at a disadvantage to the other players. In one of the tournaments, out of the frustration of losing to an inferior opponent, I slammed my racquet over my knee and broke it.

Dr. Meyer immediately suspended me from the team.

I was sent home until further notice.

Upon hearing of the incident, my mother was outraged and confronted Dr. Meyer. She threatened to bring this case before the eight-member panel of the Sports Authority and accused Dr. Meyer of abuse of power against a child.

Again, the strength of her resolve—her toughness—convinced him to back down.

Clearly rattled, he tried to blame his decision on a shortage of new racquets.

My mother refused to accept this lame excuse and persisted with her complaint. She requested a meeting before the governing panel of the Sports Authority. As the head of the Purchasing Agency, my mother knew all of the panel members and had treated them very well for years.

One might say they were among the "elites" that benefitted from her food deliveries and payoffs.

Thus, she had power over them and they knew it.

"I expect you to fix this problem or there will be drastic changes!" she threatened.

The members of the panel knew just what she meant.

Seven days later, I was invited back to the tennis camp and given two new Dunlop Max Fly racquets.

My skill as a tennis player continued to improve

exponentially. By the time I was sixteen, I was the #1 player on the Boys' tennis team and no other player came close to challenging me for that ranking. I could also beat many of the top players on the Men's tennis team.

Although our lives were controlled and monitored closely by the KGB, athletes were revered and treated like gods by the general population. We were issued special identification cards that allowed us to move to the head of any food line during any home visits. We were also encouraged to participate in international competitions where victories enhanced our status within our country, as well as the world.

But all along, we understood that we were being used as propaganda tools by the Soviet Union. Athletic dominance was just another way for the Russians to prove that communism was superior to capitalism.

I often thought of the advice from Ana and my mother, but never discussed it with anyone, not even my closest friends on the tennis team. In Communist Czechoslovakia you couldn't trust anyone with your secret desire to defect. The KGB made it clear that informants that tipped them off about such plans would be handsomely rewarded.

Offenders faced dire consequences—usually death.

The thought of this haunted me during those

moments that I considered escaping.

I could not imagine that the Russians could be so cruel to carry out the execution of a teenager.

I soon learned, however, that the depth of their cruelty had no bounds.

Chapter Five

BY THE TIME I reached my sixteenth birthday, the Boys' tennis team was recognized as one of the best teams in Europe. One of my friends on the team was Ian Novotny—a couple of years older, but very much my contemporary. Ian was also a great athlete. Not only was he highly proficient as a tennis player, he was a championship swimmer.

The city of Bratislava is the capital city of Slovakia and is located on the Danube River directly across from Austria and Hungary. The Danube serves as a natural border between the three countries. At its narrowest point, the distance across the river from Bratislava to Austria is approximately forty meters. Since Austria was not part of the post-World War II pact that created the Soviet bloc, it remained a free and independent country.

After the war, barbed wire was erected by the Russians all along the border of the Danube in Bratislava to prevent Slovakians from defecting by swimming or taking a small rowboat across the river to Austria.

The Russians also built towers along the river bank where heavily armed security guards scanned the beaches at night with floodlights looking for people that were trying to escape.

One night, without a hint of warning to me or his other friends on the team, Ian attempted to defect.

Ian planned to sneak across the beach and cut through the barbed wire between the light cycles that scanned the area after dark. Then, using a straw for breathing, he intended to swim under water for the entire distance of forty meters until he reached the shores of Austria.

Once in Austria, he would be a free man.

As an expert swimmer, he most likely felt very confident that he could remain under water for the entire distance.

His plan was somewhat ingenious, except for the lack of one vital piece of information.

Sadly, what Ian did not know was that the Russian guards used rakes to smooth over the sandy beach every day just before sunset. Anyone approaching the water after dark would leave footprints that could easily be detected by the guards when the lights in the towers shined down on the beach.

One night, during his attempted escape, Ian's

footprints in the sand were spotted by the guards in the towers.

Their lights immediately scanned the edge of the beach near the water.

The lights focused on Ian.

He had nowhere to hide.

Within seconds, the guards opened fire with machine guns.

Ian was riddled with bullets and fell dead before he reached the water.

Early the next morning the entire camp of young athletes was called to a meeting on one of the soccer fields. All of us were perplexed about the suddenness of this unexpected meeting. Some of the boys were half-asleep and still in their pajamas. We exchanged nervous and confused glances but seemed to know full well that something serious must have occurred.

An eerie silence pervaded the field.

None of us said a word.

The commander of the guards marched slowly out of guard house and stood at attention before us. He scanned the crowd of boys, seemingly looking for a reaction—someone who would make a sound or movement.

But we were frozen in our positions. No one dared to flinch or say a word.

Then the commander launched into a loud and angry tirade about Ian's attempted escape, making sure that we heard every one of the gory details—how he died and how any other attempts at escaping would be handled in a similar manner.

The news was devastating.

As I looked around, I could see that my tennis teammates and the other athletes were in a state of shock—some overcome with emotion over the loss of their friend—such a young, talented person.

The guards, on the other hand, stared at us defiantly—determined to show the powerful forces we were up against if any of us attempted to defect. Then, one by one, each athlete was questioned by the KGB guards.

Brutal intimidation tactics, of course, were employed.

Some of the younger boys cried under the pressure of this intense cross-examination.

"What do you know about this?" a guard yelled at me as he stood just inches from my face.

"Nothing," I said.

The guard became increasingly agitated. "But you were his friend. Not so? He must have said something to you!"

"No. He never said a word to me about his plan. I had no idea."

"If you're lying to me, the penalties will be severe. You'll be dropped from the team and put in prison… maybe worse. You better tell the truth now."

I said nothing.

Then he grabbed my shoulders and shouted into my face. "How is it possible that you…one of his best friends…had no idea that he was planning this escape? Maybe I should take you inside and let some of the other guards beat the truth out of you!"

Again, I looked straight into his eyes and said nothing, all the while maintaining a stoic expression while simultaneously trying to suppress my inner anger.

Frustrated by my silence and perhaps accepting the fact that I had no information to offer, he pushed me away and moved on to harass another member of the tennis team. This ordeal lasted for more than an hour and turned out to be a fruitless effort by the guards— none of the athletes in the camp had any knowledge of Ian's plans to escape.

I looked around. Some of the young boys sat on the grass, trembling and crying quietly, clearly shell-shocked by the harshness of the interrogations. The coaches came out and began to round up everyone for breakfast in the dining hall while simultaneously trying to console those younger boys that were still unable to control their emotions.

It was a sad scene, but one that only intensified my resolve.

I understood then, more than ever, that Ana and my mother were right.

I began to plan my escape to the West.

Chapter Six

SIX MONTHS LATER, the Boys' Tennis Team was notified that we were going on a European tour. All members of the team were issued a passport and given the itinerary that included a series of Junior Davis Cup competitions in several European cities, including Paris, Rome and Athens.

Prior to leaving, our Bratislava team was scheduled to play a preliminary match against the Junior Davis Cup team of Prague. My father received permission from the coaches to have a lunch meeting with me in Prague before we traveled to Paris.

My father had undergone even more changes in his political and cultural views during the years I was in the sports camp. Despite being Jewish, he had become, in many ways, a man of privilege in our Communist-controlled society. The Russians valued his knowledge and expertise in computer technology and had become more dependent upon his skills with each passing year. To show their appreciation—or perhaps to keep him under their control—they showered him with an increased package of "perks." He received a handsome salary, a nice car, and his own driver, to name but a few of his new privileges.

As a result, his political leanings had transformed and he had become a believer in the benefits of Communism. Even his social circle was comprised exclusively of fellow communists whom he often invited to our home for dinner. In order to avoid suspicion, my mother had to cook elaborate meals to entertain these guests, but she disliked them intensely.

My mother remained a steadfast opponent of Communism and a firm believer in basic tenets of a free society: freedom of speech, freedom of religion, and all the freedoms that existed in the Western World.

Thus, the political discussions—perhaps better described as "confrontations"—in the privacy of our home were often quite heated. In order to keep me out of the argument, my parents often shifted mid-sentence to another language, German or Hungarian, that I didn't understand.

Over time, my father had also abandoned many of the Jewish customs, including keeping kosher, that my mother had maintained in our house. On my home visits from the sports camp, my father would often take me out for lunch.

His usual order was a sandwich with pork or ham.

Then, before diving in with his first bite, he'd look at me with a sly smile, "Don't tell your mother."

I was surprised to see my father in Prague since, over the past few years, our relationship had become rather cold. To me, a major irritant was the fact that he, in contrast to my mother, had never attended one game of soccer or one tennis match in which I had competed.

We met at a bar/restaurant in downtown Prague.

He looked somewhat uneasy as we sat down at a small table for two.

He fidgeted with his hands and licked his lips nervously. His eyes darted around the room and he occasionally looked back over his right shoulder.

Is he afraid that someone is watching us?

Finally, he leaned closer.

"Daniel," he whispered. "You have to rethink your plans very carefully."

"What plans?"

"I know you have spoken to Ana and your mother about escaping. It's not a good idea."

"Why?"

"It's too dangerous. The KGB guards are heavily armed and much smarter than you think. Look what happened to your friend, Ian."

"But that's why I don't want to live here. I want to be free."

He shook his head. "The Communist way is not such a bad life. Look at me...they treat me very well."

"But they control you, don't they? They're not much different from the Nazis you escaped from. Isn't that so?"

The challenging tone of my voice startled him.

He didn't answer.

The subject had made him very uncomfortable.

Our brief conversation reminded me that the topic of my father's escape from a Nazi concentration camp during World War II was always "off limits." He would never discuss it. Besides his scarred finger, the only hint of his horrible experience was a conversation I overheard as a young boy when he told my mother that he had been subjected to experimental hormone injections by the Nazi doctors.

I was tempted to push our discussion forward to obtain the details of his escape, but my thought process was interrupted when the waiter brought our food.

My father jumped in immediately and changed the subject with a random thought of his own.

"Listen," he said. "Let's have a glass of beer!"

Then, looking up to the waiter, he said, "Bring two Pilsner's."

As a sixteen-year-old, I didn't know a whole lot about beer and only much later in life realized that Pilsner beer was 12% alcohol—roughly 2 ½ times stronger than regular draught beer.

The waiter returned with two bottles of Pilsner.

My father and I clicked our bottles together in a toast.

"To a great trip and winning matches," he said. "And, most of all, think carefully. Don't take any risks; come home safe."

I nodded and smiled, but did not reply.

Nothing, not even my father's warnings, could stop me from finding a way to escape. I was determined to defect whenever my best opportunity presented itself.

We finished eating and downing our Pilsner's. I was woozy as I stood up from the table, but tried to hide the effects of the alcohol from my father.

His driver picked him up outside the restaurant and they drove off. I crossed the street and hopped on a trolley to get back to the hotel and meet up with my teammates and coaches.

I began to feel more lightheaded and realized that I was actually drunk.

I wanted to sit down but all of the seats were taken. I had no choice but to stand on the edge of the aisle and grab onto a hand grip for support.

The open-sided trolley jerked forward. Suddenly I lost control of the hand grip.

I tumbled down the steps, fell off the trolley and landed on the street.

The trolley came to a screeching halt.

Several passengers ran back to help me.

They helped me to my feet and brushed off my clothes.

Fortunately, I was not hurt badly.

I got back on the trolley and held on to the hand grip more tightly until we reached the stop for my team's hotel.

I got off and walked slowly down the street to the hotel, trying carefully to avoid an occasional, but noticeable stagger in my footsteps.

When I got to my room, I collapsed into bed and slept for the rest of the day and all through the night.

The next day I played very well and we won our matches against the Prague team.

Chapter Seven

PRIOR TO LEAVING for Paris—the first leg of our trip—the team was gathered by the head of the Sports Authority and given our orders.

1. While traveling in these foreign cities, do not talk to strangers or any member of the press.
2. Do not leave the hotel or the competition area without the permission of the coaches.
3. Armed guards will be assigned to be with the team at all times. The guards will verify that each member of the team follows these orders. Those players who disobey the rules will be removed from the team and severely punished.

Although it was never stated in the orders, all of us knew that these cities were part of the free world. To ignore the orders and escape from the guards meant that the athlete was free.

Free from oppression.

Free from government control of nearly every movement.

But, if you were caught escaping, the guards made sure that you paid the ultimate price—your life would be over.

This sobering thought occupied my mind for a good part of every day.

I tried to put it aside.

No use.

I began to fear that my preoccupation with these negative thoughts would adversely affect my play on the tennis court and perhaps make the guards suspicious.

My emotions were getting the best of me.

I struggled to fight my way through each day without revealing my intentions.

During the first round of matches in Paris, I played fairly well and reached the semi-finals. The competition was stiff, and I was happy to have advanced so far.

Next, we traveled to Rome.

But, by the time we got on the courts, my mind had drifted far away from competitive tennis.

I was totally distracted.

This trip had been my first exposure to independent countries outside of Czechoslovakia and had impacted me tremendously.

There were no food lines or shortages.

People moved about freely—on beautiful streets—smiling and happy as they walked in and out of shops or sat at a sidewalk café.

There were no police or military guards watching their every movement.

All of these images were in sharp contrast to the life I knew in Communist-occupied Czechoslovakia. I realized more than ever that I could no longer live in such a repressive country, under control of a totalitarian government that required complete subservience to the state.

I became convinced that I had to take decisive action on this trip whenever the opportunity presented itself.

I wanted to be free.

Chapter Eight

ON THE PLANE ride to Athens, I carried out the first stage of my escape.

After our plane had taken off and reached cruising altitude, I unbuckled my seat belt and slumped forward in my seat. Then I grabbed the right side of my abdomen and began screaming in pain.

Everyone turned around or leaned toward the aisle to see what was happening.

Within seconds I slipped out of my seat and landed hard on the floor, in the process almost banging my head on the armrest of the seat across the aisle.

I screamed louder and desperately gasped for air.

Two flight attendants rushed toward me and began shouting questions in Italian and then Greek.

I didn't speak either language but was sure they were asking, "Is there a doctor on board?"

An older man stood up from his seat in the front of the plane and walked back toward what had become a frantic scene.

I continued playing out the drama—a teenage boy writhing in acute pain and grasping at his right side.

The man, who appeared to be in his 60s, spoke Italian and began asking questions.

His manner and take-charge approach indicated to me that he was indeed a doctor. The flight attendants replied and shrugged, indicating that they had no idea what precipitated my sudden affliction.

The doctor leaned down and asked for help in straightening my body into the middle of the aisle.

He palpated the area around my stomach and the right side of my abdomen.

I recognized his intent and screamed even louder.

I grabbed at his hand and tried to push it away.

The flight attendants attempted to restrain me, all the while yelling, "No...no!"

The doctor felt my forehead, paused for a few seconds, then stood up and walked toward the cockpit. One of the flight attendants accompanied him.

In a few minutes an announcement—in Italian, then Greek—came over the intercom system.

Two of our coaches and one of the guards moved me from the aisle to the floor of the galley area of the plane. One of the flight attendants lifted my head so I could take a sip from a cup of water.

The head coach leaned down toward me. "The

pilot just told everyone that they've radioed ahead for an ambulance to meet us when we land," he said. "They're gonna take you to a hospital. Looks like you have appendicitis,"

I nodded but said nothing other than continuing with a steady moan and an occasional painful outburst.

I had accomplished the first phase of my escape plan, but had no idea how I could pull off the next.

Chapter Nine

THE PLANE LANDED and I was immediately placed on a stretcher, wheeled to the ambulance and taken to Athens Hospital. At the hospital, I received a complete barrage of medical tests: x-rays, urine sample, blood tests, etc.

Not to my surprise, the doctors determined that I did not have appendicitis.

The doctors, recognizing that I did not understand their language, huddled with my coaches in a corner of the emergency room and spoke to them through an interpreter.

After a few minutes, one of my coaches came over to my gurney.

"Daniel," he said. "The doctors think you had some sort of acute gas attack … maybe a reaction to some food you ate? Maybe food poisoning? They don't know for sure. But they're gonna give you some IV fluids and some antacid medication. They think you should go back home."

"Okay," I said.

"So, we'll have to assign two guards to take you back to Bratislava. They'll take you to the airport after the doctors are done here. My guess is you'll be on a flight tonight."

"Alright."

My mind began racing.

Two guards… trained by the KGB and armed with guns. Taking me back to the airport where there are more security guards and restricted areas. How will this work? If I try to get away, will the Greek authorities help me or merely turn me over to the Communist guards?

Now, for the first time, I became really scared.

Perspiration formed on my forehead.

My heart pounded with anticipation.

I tried to appear disinterested as I lay on the gurney waiting for the IV to finish.

Everything ahead of me was a frightening unknown.

My mind became blank.

The nurses disconnected my IV, placed a bandage on my arm and handed some paperwork to two guards that had walked into my room. I had seen these two during our trip but had never had any contact with either one. They were not the guards I often spotted at our sports camp.

The guard who seemed to be in charge was a man in his late forties—tall, about 6′1″. He took the papers from the nurse, never smiled and walked over to the chair where I sat.

"Come on," he said. "Put on your jacket and let's go. We're going back to the airport."

The other guard was younger—probably in his thirties—but he was a short, chubby guy. My first instinct was that, if I started running, I'd be five steps ahead of him in seconds and he'd never be able to catch me.

But the gun on his hip served as a grim reminder that he might not waste time chasing after me.

Why would he?

Letting me escape would put his own life in jeopardy; shooting me would likely earn a promotion.

We got into a taxi and began the drive to the airport.

The older guard sat in the front seat. I sat in the back with the chubby one. After a few minutes, the older guard looked at his watch and mumbled something to the driver. The driver nodded, exchanged a few words with the guard, and then made a turn off the main highway.

"The Athena Restaurant is just a few minutes from the airport," the older guard said as he turned toward us. "I've eaten there before; it's a great place. We've got more than two hours to kill before our flight. The driver will take us there and come back to pick us up later."

The chubby one smiled. "Sounds good to me. I'm starving!"

Then he looked over to me. "You hungry, kid? Are you able to eat?"

I shrugged. Said nothing.

There was no way I wanted to arouse suspicion about my "illness" by diving into a big meal. Besides, food was the last thing on my mind.

I needed a plan and had to come up with something pretty quickly.

I knew that my only chance to escape would occur in that restaurant.

I tried to remain calm so I could think clearly.

But my anxiety level was peaking.

My heart rate quickened.

Within a few minutes the taxi pulled up in front of the restaurant and dropped us off. I didn't know what town we were in. But, judging from what the guards had said to each other, I assumed it was a small suburb outside of Athens.

The lead guard looked at his watch and spoke to the driver through the front passenger window. "See you in about an hour and fifteen minutes," he said.

The cab drove away.

The chubby guard took me by the arm and led me to the front door just beneath a large sign—Athena Restaurant. I could tell by the way he held my arm that he fully intended to keep me from getting too far away.

Does he know what I'm thinking?

The words of the big guard kept repeating in my head … *"an hour and fifteen minutes."*

That's all the time I had to make my move.

If I make a mistake, my life could be over in an hour.

Chapter Ten

BEFORE WE WALKED into the restaurant, I glanced around to get a sense of the area. It was a general suburban business area—some small shops, a drug store, another restaurant across the street—nothing that would offer safe haven or a means of transportation to take me far away from the guards.

Besides, I had no money—in particular, no Greek currency—to even pay bus fare.

A feeling of desperation came over me.

I could be screwed.

If I was taken back to Bratislava and shown to have no medical diagnosis, I'd be interrogated by Dr. Meyer. He was a despicable character, but he wasn't stupid. He'd figure out that I had faked an injury. Maybe even suspect that I was planning to defect?

The consequences flashed through my mind.

The penalties against me and my parents could be severe.

Maybe imprisonment.

Maybe worse.

The Communists had spent years and untold amounts of money to train young athletes like me to further their agenda for world dominance through the symbolism of athletic superiority. They couldn't afford to merely discourage defectors; they had to crush them as well as any family members that may have assisted in the effort.

The very thought of the repercussions chilled me.

We walked into the restaurant and were seated at a square table for four.

I tried to slow down my breathing and keep my eyes from darting around at the interior. If I appeared nervous or to be casing the place, for sure I'd put these two guys on high alert.

I needed them to relax and catch them at a weak moment.

Barely half of the tables were occupied. The only door I saw was the main front door through which we had entered.

Is there no other way out of this place? There has to be!

A waiter came over with menus and poured water into our glasses. The older guard immediately spoke up, "Double vodka on the rocks."

"Make it two!" chimed in the chubby one.

The waiter looked at me.

I waved him off, content to just continue sipping my water.

A few minutes later, the waiter returned with a basket of pita bread and the drinks. The guards pounded down the vodka within minutes while I took a few bites of a piece of pita bread.

The waiter returned to take their dinner order—the house lamb Shish Kebob Special—and, of course, another round of double vodkas.

As they drank their second round, they seemed to loosen up quite a bit.

The older guard smiled at me. "So...when you were in Rome, did you meet any nice Italian girls?"

"No. We didn't have a chance to walk around on our own. After practices or the competition, we usually just went back to the hotel."

"How about back home? You have a girlfriend there?"

The chubby guard laughed.

"No," I said. "I'm only allowed to go home once every thirty days."

The chubby guard winced.

Then, with an apologetic tone, the older guard said, "Don't worry. If you become a tennis star, then you'll meet lots of girls."

I let it pass.

Their dinners arrived and they dove into the food.

The older guard signaled to the waiter and held up his empty vodka glass.

Within minutes, another round of double vodkas was on the table.

With each round I noticed that their laughter became more boisterous, their words became slurred, and they began to yawn.

The alcohol had taken full effect.

These two guys were beyond being tipsy; they were totally smashed.

I knew the taxi driver would be returning shortly to take us to the airport. I had to make a move now or my opportunity would be lost.

I sat up in my chair and looked over to the older guard. "I have to go to the bathroom."

The chubby guard ignored me and kept eating.

The older one glanced up at me and then looked to the other guard. "You better go with him."

The chubby one shrugged and, while still chewing, raised his hands in frustration and asked, "What the fuck am I supposed to do … hold it for him? He's sixteen years old..."

The older guard cut him off and shot a stern look across the table.

"No! You better go with him. Stand outside and watch the door."

Officer "Chubbs" finished chewing, swallowed his food, grabbed his cloth napkin and wiped off his face. He stood up from his chair and made a backhanded motion for me to head toward the rest room while he followed behind. As we left the table, out of the corner of my eye, I saw him reach to his waist to feel the gun in its holster.

Was that a simple reflex reaction or was he sending a message?

We got to the restroom, and I reached out and opened the door.

He peeked in over my shoulder and then motioned for me to go in alone.

I went in.

Thank God it's a single occupant bathroom!

I pushed the button on the knob to engage the lock.

The bathroom was small—a urinal and a hand-washing sink on the left side of a toilet stall.

I opened the door of the toilet stall.

Above the toilet, a horizontal awning window, hinged at the top, was partially open.

This was my chance!

I went into the stall and climbed up on the toilet seat. I began pushing on the window to force it upward and out to open it to its maximum. But the slide mechanism was old and rusty.

The window hardly budged.

I pulled myself up higher to get greater leverage on the window.

It barely moved.

I tried again.

Still, it barely moved.

I've got to get this window open!

By this time my heart rate was out of control.

Sweat rolled off my forehead.

Then several knocks on the door startled me.

"Hey… what's going on in there? You can't take all day!" the guard yelled.

"I'll be out in a few minutes," I said.

I became frantic.

My desperation caused my adrenaline to kick in.

With a burst of energy and all of my strength, I pushed the window wide open.

Thank God!

Then I stood on top of the toilet tank and pulled myself upward until I was able to get my head and upper torso to lean out and face the ground below.

But I was stuck.

The opening is too small. I'll never fit through it!

I knew there was no turning back.

It was now or never.

I took a deep breath, grabbed the side edges of the window frame and mustered all of my strength to pull upward.

With a final powerful thrust, I pushed against the sides of the building and forced my body up and out through the window.

I landed with a thud—chest first—on the ground below.

The impact of hitting the ground stunned me, and I lost my breath for a few seconds.

I gasped for air.

My arms and hips were bleeding from cuts and deep scratches that happened when I pulled myself through the narrow window opening.

My shirt—soaked with perspiration—was also stained with blood, grass and dirt.

My tennis shorts were torn at the pockets.

But I had no time to take complete inventory of the damage. My instinct for survival took over immediately. In near panic, I got to my feet and began running.

The years of exercise and endurance training kicked my legs into high gear.

I sprinted away from the restaurant and kept running.

Chapter Eleven

AS I RAN, I kept zig-zagging away from street lights, trying to shield myself from detection by staying in the darker areas as much as possible. I looked off into the distance before me—toward the lights of the Acropolis, high above the city of Athens.

Athens was miles away—I had no idea how many.

But I was determined to get there by running without stopping.

I settled into a steady pace, trying to avoid running out of energy too soon and collapsing with muscle cramps. As I ran, I thought of my two half-brothers who I had never met—killed by the Nazis in a concentration camp.

Did they have a chance to escape?

Somehow, I felt that they would have encouraged me to do so.

I was also running for my mother.

She was a strong, determined woman—a true role model for me. I did not want her to face the loss of another son.

So, I kept running.

I thought of my friend, Ian—shot and killed by the KGB while trying to escape.

A young life snuffed out by heartless people.

If he were still alive, I knew he would be right beside me—running for freedom.

So, I kept running.

I thought of my father.

Was our last conversation an attempt to sway me into believing in Communism?

Or did he recognize the extreme danger for a sixteen-year-old who tried to defect?

Was our toast over a glass of Pilsner his subtle attempt to keep me alive?

In some ways, these thoughts motivated me.

I began to feel that I was running in honor of all of them.

There was no way I could stop.

I had to stay alive.

Suddenly a siren sounded behind me.

I panicked, dove down behind a large bush and landed in a muddy patch of grass.

I scrambled to keep my head down and stay out of sight.

My heart pounded and my body trembled.

A police car—lights flashing, sirens blaring—

whizzed by without stopping.

Are they looking for me?

I delayed for a few minutes to make sure the police car had not circled back toward me.

Nothing.

I got up and resumed running.

My white tennis clothes had become splattered with even more patches of mud.

I didn't even bother to brush them off.

I kept running.

I tried to get control of my emotions—this feeling of paranoia that the guards were chasing me with a complete battalion of armed soldiers.

But, after a while, I began to think more clearly.

They had no vehicle.

Were they likely to hire a taxi to cruise around for hours looking for a getaway kid?

I doubted it.

If they went to the Greek authorities, could they enlist their help in tracking down a defector so they could take him back to Communist-occupied Czechoslovakia and execute him?

I didn't think so.

But, then again, I was sixteen and totally unfamiliar with international laws.

Maybe the guards could say I got lost and they were

trying to find me?

Would the police buy that story?

I didn't know.

My best option was to keep running.

And that's just what I did.

I ran and ran and ran.

I didn't have a wristwatch, so my only way to judge the time was to wait until sunrise.

I kept running through the darkness—street by street, always toward the city lights of Athens, but constantly looking back over my shoulder to check for a car that might be pursuing me.

My pacing became rhythmical—steadier and more efficient as I seemed to breeze through the miles.

After a few hours, however, my legs began to ache and my throat became parched.

My mouth had gone dry.

I ran my tongue across my teeth and sucked my cheeks inward, trying to moisten them.

Nothing worked.

I desperately needed water.

But here, on these strange streets, in the middle of the night, there was nowhere to find it.

I was fighting against so many negative sensations and emotions—fear, hunger, thirst, my aching legs—but I tried to ignore them.

I just kept running.

As I got closer to Athens, I passed more indications that I was nearing the center of the city.

The streets were wider.

The stores—all closed—were larger.

But then I saw something very important.

A telephone booth!

Standing right on the corner of this street!

I rushed into it, took the receiver off the hook, and began rapidly moving the hook up and down to get the attention of an operator. Finally, a woman's voice came through the receiver.

"Help…help…," I pleaded. I began to alternate my language between Russian and Slovakian, hoping she could understand me. "I defected from Czechoslovakia and I need to get in touch with the US Embassy!"

The operator began answering me, but she only spoke Greek.

She could not understand Russian or Slovakian.

I was getting nowhere.

Eventually, she disconnected me.

The line was dead.

Frustrated, I slammed the receiver back on the hook.

I continued to hold the receiver in my right hand as I leaned forward and supported my body against the telephone booth with my left.

My head dropped down.

My eyes welled up with tears.

The frustration and uncertainty of my future had overwhelmed me.

I was on the verge of total exhaustion.

I need help. But I have nowhere to find it.

Seconds later, I heard a loud siren.

Immediately, I dropped down—practically on my knees—to the floor of the telephone booth.

Another police car roared past. Its blue and red lights flashed so brightly—near blinding in intensity— that they lit up the entire area, including the telephone booth where I huddled in fear.

I was scared to death.

The sound of the siren slowly faded away.

The police car never stopped.

Am I being hunted? Or is this all in my mind?

I was becoming unglued.

I got back on my feet and looked around.

No one in sight.

I forced myself to resume running.

You can't stop! You can't let them capture you!

Every stride had become a struggle.

The time passed.

Dawn was approaching.

In some ways, the darkness of night had afforded a

strange feeling of security. I knew it would be harder to stay unnoticed in broad daylight.

What if the police had been notified to be on the "look out" for a teenage runaway? How could I explain my situation without knowing their language?

My mind swirled with wild possibilities.

My only chance to survive was to stay on the move.

I kept running toward the center of Athens but veered off to a more diagonal direction, away from the path of the police car that had just passed.

My inner clock and the imminent sunrise told me that I had been running and hiding for more than six hours.

I needed food and water but still had no way to obtain either one.

I kept running.

Just after sunrise, I spotted a man—medium height and a full beard—leaning over to open the locks of a dry-cleaning store. He appeared to be struggling with the locks and didn't notice as I approached.

I stopped on the sidewalk a few feet away.

After running all night and being forced, at times, to hide on the ground behind bushes, my body was muddied and scratched, and I was dripping in sweat.

I was a mess.

He looked up from his door and stepped back in a double-take.

"What the hell!! Is this kid going to rob me?" is what he must have thought.

"I need help," I said.

My voice cracked with emotion. "Please…please help me."

The look of fear on his face softened.

He smiled weakly and nodded.

"I'll be happy to help you," he said.

I nearly cried when I heard those words because they were spoken in perfect Russian.

Russian!

Of more than two million people living in Athens, Greece in 1964, what were the chances that the first person I met spoke fluent Russian?

Within minutes he took me inside his dry-cleaning store and gave me some food and water that were stored in a small refrigerator in his back office. He also provided a few towels so I could clean up.

He listened intently as I told my story. He had read about the atrocities and oppression in the Soviet Bloc countries, but mine was the only firsthand account he had ever heard.

As a safety precaution, he asked me to stay in his back office—out of sight from any of his customers or visitors—until 8:00 AM.

Precisely at eight o'clock, he called the United

States Embassy in Athens to inform them that I had defected from Communist-occupied Czechoslovakia.

The fear and desperation that had consumed my every thought less than twelve hours earlier had been replaced with pure joy and excitement.

I thought I was home free…that my problems were over.

But I had no idea of the pain and heartache that awaited just ahead.

Chapter Twelve

WITHIN AN HOUR, two officers from the CIA arrived and drove me to the United States embassy.

My half-sister, Ana, had relocated from Tel Aviv to New York City so a staff member at the embassy was able to obtain her contact information. They placed a trans-continental call to her and put me on the phone.

"Moishe!" she screamed excitedly. "You are free! I am so proud and happy for you!"

I was speechless.

Hearing her voice caused me to choke up. Tears began to stream down my face.

The culmination of the stressful events of the past twenty-four hours had taken my breath away.

My body trembled.

My emotions let loose.

I began to cry.

"Moishe? Can you hear me?"

I tried to speak but I couldn't reply.

"Moishe? Are you okay?" she pleaded.

"Yes," I blurted out.

But I was overcome by emotion and turned the handset back to the embassy agent.

"He's fine, Ana," he said. "Just a bit emotional after what he's been through. We'll be in touch with you once we make arrangements for his trip to New York. In the meantime, call us if you have any questions."

The call ended.

The agent reached over and patted my shoulders.

"Don't worry. We'll contact HIAS. You're in good hands now. We'll make sure you are safe."

Chapter Thirteen

SEVERAL HOURS LATER, one of the senior adminis-trators at the US Embassy asked to speak to me in his office.

"Daniel, how are you holding up? Has everyone here been helpful?" he asked, through an interpreter who spoke Russian.

"Yes. Everyone has been so nice to me."

"That's great. I have some good news for you. Through HIAS we've found a Greek family that would like to host you—let you live with them—until you're ready to go to the United States. They live just outside of Athens. He's a doctor...," he said, as he stopped for a few seconds to look down at his notes. "Oh yes ... Stefano Assisopolous and his wife, Maria."

I nodded and waited for him to continue.

"While you are living there, someone from our of-fice will pick you up every morning and take you to a school where you can begin to learn English. If you are going to be living and going to school in the US, you will need to speak English. So, this will be a great opportunity for you to get started. HIAS will also provide you with a small allowance so you'll have some spending money in Athens before you depart for the US. Athens is a great city! While you are here, you should take advantage and enjoy it."

I was thrilled.

In a short time, I was driven to the home of Dr. and Mrs. Stefano Assisopolous, a couple in their mid-60s. They were very kind and gentle people that treated me extremely well. They provided me with my own bedroom, food, some new clothing, and, most importantly, the security of knowing that I was in a safe environment.

However, because they were a couple with very busy professional lives, I hardly saw them. Most mornings I woke up to an empty house. This was not, in itself, a big problem since the refrigerator was always well-stocked with food, milk and fresh juice.

But it was a bit strange for me, as a sixteen-year-old who had always been surrounded by a large group of peers at the Sports Camp in Bratislava and on road trips with my tennis teammates.

I learned to adjust and rely on the sound of an alarm clock rather than the harsh wake-up commands of the KGB guards. To this day, the morning commotion of my days in the Sports Camp dormitory remains well-etched in my memory.

A woman from the US Embassy picked me up every weekday morning and dropped me off at a school where I took English classes. At first, I was excited for the opportunity to learn to speak English.

But I struggled mightily.

As a young boy in Czechoslovakia, I had no trouble learning to speak Russian in elementary school after primarily speaking Slovakian in my home for the first five years of my life.

English, however, was so much harder for me.

None of the rules seemed to make sense.

The three hours of classes every day became a real drag and I made little progress. I began to wonder if I could get by in the United States without ever developing command of the English language.

But I soon learned to put these negative thoughts in perspective.

At home in Czechoslovakia, the Communists controlled nearly every facet of my life—where I went to school, when I could play and practice tennis, what I ate, when I could see my parents ... the list goes on and on.

In contrast, the freedom I experienced during my ninety days in Athens was exhilarating. My afternoons were a complete pleasure. I usually walked through the Acropolis Food Market and enjoyed a nice lunch. I loved sampling the wide variety of new food—moussaka, souvlaki, gyro sandwiches on fresh pita bread, and delicious desserts such as baklava and feta me meli.

I also visited the large variety of shops and historical landmarks in Athens. I even had the opportunity to play tennis at a private club just outside of the main city.

Everyone in Czechoslovakia knew that they were always just one wrong step away from being in trouble, imprisoned, or even worse. The stress of this uncertainty wore heavily on the mind of every citizen.

For me, now far removed from that environment, the taste of my new-found freedom was very sweet.

I couldn't wait to get to the United States.

Chapter Fourteen

DURING MY TIME in Athens, I was able to speak to Ana on five different occasions, thanks to the staff at the US Embassy. I had two options for my trip to the United States—by plane directly to New York or by passenger ship on a fourteen-day cruise with stops at various European countries along the way.

I was anxious to get to New York, so I initially opted for the travel by air. Ana, however, highly recommended the cruise.

"Moishe," she said. "When will you have such a great opportunity to see all of these beautiful countries again? Take advantage of this time in your life to visit some of the European historical sites and experience the culture of other parts of the free world."

I listened and ultimately took her advice.

After ninety days in Athens, on a mild summer day, August 25, 1964, I boarded an Italian passenger ship, the Lorenzo Marcello, and began my journey to New York. The US Embassy, with funding provided by HIAS, made the arrangements for my passage.

My living quarters were far from first class accommodations. In fact, I was given a bunk in the lowest area of the ship commonly referred to as "steerage." As a former inhabitant of one of the "spartan" dormitory rooms at the Sports Camp, this bare-bones cabin was not really a hardship. In fact I now view it as a significant improvement.

Besides, it was only for a short term; I was on my way to New York!

As soon as the ship departed Athens for the fourteen-day cruise, I took the precaution of hiding my important papers. These papers included verification of my identity, my birth records, my past history living in Communist-occupied Czechoslovakia, and certification from the US Embassy to guarantee my admission to the United States under the 1951 Convention Related to the Status of Refugees Seeking Asylum.

While I was alone in the cabin, I carefully placed these papers in a large envelope which I hid between the blanket and sheets on the underside of the mattress on my bed.

My roommate was a young guy—Julio Lopez—age nineteen, from Cuba. He was about 6' 1" with a muscular, athletic build. I eventually found out he was a wrestler who had been in Greece for a wrestling competition and was on his way to the United States for another wrestling event in Iowa.

Julio was friendly enough, but the problem for us was that he could only speak Spanish. I spoke three languages—Russian, Slovakian and English, the latter in which I was still hardly fluent. For the first two days, therefore, our communication was basically limited to hand signals and smiles.

Fortunately, we met another traveler on the ship who stayed in a neighboring cabin. Yugo Dubozniak, age 29, spoke Spanish, Russian and English. Julio and I immediately latched onto Yugo since he served as our translator. As a result of this need to communicate, the three of us became friends and hung around together for most of the trip.

The Lorenzo Marcello made several stops at European ports on its way to New York. Our first ports were in Italy—Palermo, Naples, Florence and Genoa—where additional passengers boarded the ship. Although we only spent several hours in each city, I found that each had its own charm and character.

Ana's advice was certainly well-taken: I was loving this opportunity to experience different parts of the free world.

By far, the most exciting port was our next stop—Barcelona. The shops and the flea market were beyond anything I had ever experienced. Food and produce—grapes, bananas, cheeses—and specialty meats such as kielbasa, that were scarce in Czechoslovakia, were abundant in Barcelona. I bought several shirts at the flea market and practically gorged myself sampling the wide variety of food in the marketplace.

From Barcelona we traveled to Lisbon, another great city on the Iberian Peninsula. Having lived in Bratislava where sportswear and casual clothing from western countries were not available, if not actually forbidden, I couldn't resist the sidewalk shops that sold low-priced, brand-name tee shirts, sweaters and sports caps.

I became the proverbial "kid in the candy store," loving every minute.

I bought a turtleneck sweater and wore it almost daily for the rest of the voyage.

Our next port—Halifax, Nova Scotia—involved a long trip across the Atlantic Ocean in a northwesterly direction. The beautiful, sunny weather of Europe gave way to rainy, frigid temperatures. We encountered very rough seas and were advised to stay in our cabin for the entire day. Despite the cold weather that I had experienced in my home country during the winters, I can never remember being as cold as the day we arrived in Halifax. To make matters worse, besides the sweater I bought in Lisbon, I did not have clothing suitable for winter weather.

I wrapped myself in a warm blanket and stayed in my cabin all day.

After our ship left Halifax and began to travel further south toward New York, the weather became more tolerable. Despite the warmer temperature, my two travel companions, Julio and Yugo, and I occupied most of our time in the ship's game rooms.

Chapter Fifteen

TWO DAYS BEFORE our scheduled arrival in New York, I was alone in our cabin and checked, as I did nearly every day, to verify that my papers were still safe in my hiding place. I lifted the mattress slightly and slid my hand underneath to feel the slight bulge of the large envelope tucked between the blanket and sheets.

I felt nothing.

I must be mistaken!

I blindly slid my hand all around thinking that the envelope may have been displaced toward the center of the bed.

Still nothing.

I felt all over the underside of the mattress to no avail.

In a near panic, I tore off the sheets and blanket and threw them down on the floor.

I lifted the mattress and looked between the mattress and box spring in the hope that the envelope had gotten caught somewhere on the bed frame.

I even crawled along the floor to see if the envelope had slipped inside the small space between the dresser and the wall.

Nothing!

I beame frantic.

My mind began racing.

My eyes darted around the room in disbelief.

The envelope with my important papers—the papers I needed to clear through United States Customs in just two days—was missing.

Chapter Sixteen

I BOLTED OUT of my cabin in a flash and headed to the main deck on the ship. I passed one of the ship's junior officers and stopped.

"Where is the captain?" I asked, in my best, but still quite broken English. "I need to see him."

"He's in his office. Is there an emergency?"

I began crying—nearly hysterical.

"Yes. I've been robbed. My travel documents have been stolen."

The young officer immediately sensed the urgency of the matter and escorted me to Captain John Petrocelli's office.

He knocked gently.

A voice from inside called out, "Yes? Come in, please."

The young officer opened the door and led me by the arm as we walked into the office.

"Captain, sir," he said. "We have a problem. This young man's travel documents have been stolen from his cabin."

Captain Petrocelli, a distinguished-looking man in his 60s, stood up and pointed to a chair in front of his desk.

"Come in, come in," he said. "Sit down and tell me what happened."

I explained my situation and the reason for my trip to the United States. I was choked-up with emotions but was able to describe the manner in which I had carefully hidden the large manilla envelope with my documents underneath the mattress and how I had verified its presence almost daily.

He listened intently.

"Were you always alone when you checked for the envelope?" he asked.

"Yes. I always waited until my roommate was out of the cabin. No one was ever with me."

"Is there a chance that you may have moved the envelope to another hiding place and may have just forgotten? We all do things like that. It's one of those quirks of human nature."

"No," I said. "I never moved that envelope. There was really no other place in the cabin for me to hide it."

He paused for a few seconds and looked away.

Then he suddenly looked back at me as if struck by

an important thought.

"Did you and your roommate always keep the cabin locked?"

"Always. The ship has hundreds of passengers. People are passing by in the hallway all day long."

He nodded.

"Give me some time to do a bit of an investigation. Don't discuss this with anyone … not even your roommate. Don't worry. We'll find that envelope before we dock in New York."

Chapter Seventeen

I WENT BACK to my cabin and sat on the edge of the bed. I was totally despondent, once again unsure of my future.

Fortunately, Julio and Yugo had left our floor earlier to go up to the main deck and sit on the lounge chairs on the starboard side of the ship. Their absence made it easy for me to follow the captain's orders and avoid talking to anyone.

Besides, I had no interest in socializing until I knew what had happened to my papers.

The stress of this ordeal had exhausted me.

I rested my head on the pillow of the bed, gradually closed my eyes and fell asleep.

I was awakened by several loud knocks on the door.

Whoever was there was persistent in making sure I responded.

I glanced at my watch. I had been asleep for almost two hours!

I got out of bed and walked over to the door.

"Who's there?" I asked.

"It's Captain Petrocelli, Daniel. I have something for you."

I opened the door to see the captain standing in the doorway with a big smile on his face. He was holding the large manilla envelope with my travel documents.

"Here you go, Daniel. I believe this envelope is the one you've been looking for. All right if I come in while you check to make sure nothing is missing?"

I was ecstatic.

The captain came in and stood by as I checked through all of my documents.

The papers were not in the same order as I had organized them, but everything was there. The change in order indicated that someone else had gone through these papers.

"Where did you find them?" I asked.

"In Julio's backpack."

His words stunned me.

"Julio?" I asked. "I can't believe it! Juliio?"

"Yes. I brought him into my office for questioning when we found him on the main deck. Since your cabin was always locked, he was the only person who had access besides you. Once I explained that there were severe penalties for theft of this kind, as well as the fact that, as Captain, I had the authority to conduct a thorough search of everything in your cabin, he confessed. The envelope was stashed in his backpack under a sweatshirt."

I shook my head, finding it hard to accept this story of blatant dishonesty by someone I had regarded as a friend.

"What happens to him now?" I asked.

"I'll move him to a secure cabin upstairs where he'll be detained until we dock in New York."

"I don't understand," I said. "Why would he steal my papers?"

"Official identification documents that are certified to grant asylum and an ultimate pathway to citizenship in the United States are very valuable. They are highly marketable and can be sold for a lot of money. Julio had his own documents, but he was interested in selling yours."

I didn't know what to say.

I had never been deceived in such a heinous manner—a crime that could have caused severe complications to my immigration status when I arrived in the United States.

The captain sensed my shock at these revelations and spoke to me in a calm and reassuring manner.

"Daniel," he said. "I have a suggestion that should give you some peace of mind for the rest of our trip.

Come up to my office and put your documents into the ship's safe. They will be secure, and I will personally give them to you before you disembark and proceed to US Customs in New York."

I heaved a huge sigh and said, "Thank you so much."

I never heard whether Julio Lopez faced any criminal charges, sanctions or penalties for stealing my documents.

In fact, I never saw him again.

Chapter Eighteen

FOR THE LAST two days of our cruise, I pretty much stayed by myself. At times, I sat on the main deck in a lounge chair or in the library where I could glance through copies of **Life** or **Look**, both magazines that featured pictures of movie stars and the beautiful scenery of the United States.

During these idle hours, my thoughts often turned back to the night I escaped from the Greek restaurant. I wondered what had happened to the two guards when they reported my defection to their senior officers.

In Bratislava, we always heard stories that the guards, themselves, were under intense pressure and threats from their superiors to never allow anyone to sneak across the border to Austria. Commercial vehicles and trucks that had brought food products or building supplies into Czechoslovakia were stopped and searched thoroughly as they left to verify that no one was being smuggled out of the country.

In contrast, these same vehicles had been searched

on their way into the country to make sure that they were not smuggling weapons into Czechoslovakia. One of the main fears of the Communist-controlled government was that the citizenry would become armed with guns and rifles to support a rebellion against their oppressive regime.

Any breakdown in this security mandate was blamed on the guards. Thus, despite the prestige and perks associated with being a guard for the government, the position carried a certain level of risk that could not be denied.

I assumed that the senior officer that had been assigned to take me back to Bratislava would have tried to place the blame for my escape on his chubby sidekick—the one who had been dispatched by his superior to guard the bathroom door.

But I doubted whether the argument of the senior officer would have been accepted. After all, they both had been assigned a specific duty: escort a sixteen-year-old athlete under armed guard back to Bratislava and deliver him to Dr. Meyer, the head of the Sports Camp.

The Russians viewed me simply as a commodity in which they had invested a considerable amount of time and money. From their standpoint, these two guards had been derelict in their duty by allowing this valuable commodity to escape.

Such failures could not be tolerated.

From the Russians' viewpoint, a message had to be sent to other members of the KGB and the Communist-Slovakian military that there was a price to be paid for such failures. The penalty was often years of hard labor in a Siberian labor camp or, in many cases, death by firing squad.

At times, I felt pangs of guilt that my actions had probably resulted in the demise of both guards. I usually got over these feelings by thinking back to the harsh, cold reality of the night I escaped through the restaurant window. If the two guards had rushed outside to the back of the restaurant and had seen me running away—knowing full well that they could not catch up to me—they would have shot and killed me.

Without hesitation.

With no mercy.

That night, I had no time to think of the ramifications to the guards.

I had to run.

Did I really have a choice?

While these random thoughts often raced through my mind as a teenager, little did I know that seven years later, the fate of the two guards would be revealed to me by a most unlikely source.

Chapter Nineteen

FINALLY, THE DAY arrived! Captain Petrocelli announced that we would be docking at New York's Passenger Ship Terminal around 10:00 AM.

I rushed to the deck to get a good look of the sights and scenes surrounding our arrival.

In Ana's phone calls while I was in Athens, she had assured me that she would be at the Terminal waiting to greet me.

I could hardly contain my excitement.

As the Lorenzo Marcello slowly moved forward through the morning haze, the New York skyline came into view.

I had never seen so many tall buildings clustered together.

It was a breathtaking sight.

As the ship moved forward and the haze continued to lift away, the Statue of Liberty gradually appeared on the port side. The passengers that had gathered on the deck rushed to the railings to get a first glimpse.

It seemed like the entire ship had suddenly come to attention.

A loud cheer broke out as many of the passengers began to yell, "America! ... America!"

Men, women and children began to cry and hug each other in what became a spontaneous and boisterous celebration.

The excitement of the moment was contagious.

My emotions—overwhelmed by the events and uncertainty of the past three months—let loose.

I began to cry uncontrollably.

But they were tears of pure joy.

An exhilarating feeling came over me.

Yes! I am in the United States and yes, I am finally free!

Chapter Twenty

THE LORENZO MARCELLO docked in New York harbor at noon on September 4, 1964.

I had gathered my belongings well in advance of our landing. All I had was one small duffel bag of clothes and an over-the-shoulder knapsack. Captain Petrocelli had dutifully retrieved the envelope with my important papers from the ship's safe and made sure I had that envelope in my hand as I disembarked from the ship.

I turned to wave to him as I walked down the ramp. He waved his hand and smiled broadly, much like an excited parent sending their child off on a new adventure.

I will never forget his kindness and guidance during one of the most trying experiences of my life.

The process of going through Customs and Immigration was tedious and time-consuming—partly because of the volume of foreign passengers and, in particular, because I still did not have full command of the English language. The customs agents, however, were very helpful.

After three hours, I finally completed the entire process.

Ana, her husband, Oscar, and their son, Martin waited for me in the receiving area.

When I walked through that door, I was greeted with a joyful scream from Ana, followed by hugs, much laughter and, of course, some tears.

It was an exciting, emotional reunion—the culmination of nearly one year of tension and uncertainty. For Ana, it had been an agonizing period of waiting and worrying. She had feared for my safety and had prayed that her advice to me would not have ended in a tragic, deadly failure. She also had no forewarning of my plans to defect and had been totally shocked when she received the phone call from the United States Embassy in Athens stating that I was safely in their custody.

Upon arrival at their home, I asked Ana to place an overseas call to my parents so I could speak to them and let them know I had arrived in the United States.

"No, Moishe," she said. "It is not possible to contact them. By this time, the military guards and the KGB have been to the house to interrogate them. I'm sure they are being watched closely hoping to determine your whereabouts. For all the Russians know, you could still be somewhere in Europe where they could attempt to recapture you. They view defectors as an insult, as well as a threat to their system of government. They'd like nothing better than to bring you back to Bratislava and make an example of you for the entire town to see."

"But my mother and father must be worried," I said.

She smiled.

"Don't worry ... I have a way to get a message to our mother."

Several days went by.

The subject was never brought up again.

At breakfast one morning, I slouched forward at the table trying to get fully awake before heading to school.

Ana looked over to me. "Our mother knows you are here."

Her words threw me.

I sat up in my chair.

"How does she know?" I asked, hardly able to control my excitement. "Did you send a message to her?"

With a wry look on her face, she answered, "Yes, in an indirect way ...I did send a message to her. But I know she received it."

I was puzzled.

Ana continued.

"I sent the message to her sister, Aunt Helena. You know that Mother speaks to Aunt Helena nearly every day."

"What did the message say?" I asked.

"The goods have arrived in New York."

Then she winked.

I leaned back and smiled.

I knew that, four thousand miles away in Bratislava, my mother and father were also smiling.

Chapter Twenty-One

ANA AND OSCAR lived in a single-family, two-bedroom house in the Queens borough of New York City. Martin was twelve years old and occupied the second bedroom. In anticipation of my arrival, Oscar had remodeled the basement and created a bedroom for me.

I was grateful and appreciative of my new home.

Within a few days I began classes as a sophomore student at Francis Lewis High School on Utopia Parkway, Fresh Meadows, NY. I took five English classes every day and did my best to assimilate into life in America.

Fortunately, my high school classmates were very supportive and welcomed me to their school. Of course, my status with them was greatly enhanced by my performance as an athlete for their school. By the end of my first year at Francis Lewis High School I was undefeated during the regular tennis season and suffered my only loss in the finals for the state championship. I also played varsity soccer and led the team in goals scored.

Ana and Oscar treated me very well while I lived with them. Ana did my laundry and made sure I had clean clothes for school. After the first time she washed the turtleneck sweater that I had bought in Lisbon, she walked downstairs and tapped on my bedroom door.

She held the sweater and had a mischievous look in her eyes.

"Where did you buy this piece of garbage?" she asked.

I looked up at the sweater, which had shrunk to about one-half of its former size.

"In the marketplace in Lisbon," I said.

We burst out laughing.

That was the day I learned to be careful when buying "knock-offs" from street merchants.

During my time living with Ana and her family, I developed a close relationship with Martin who looked up to me more as an older brother than an uncle.

To this day, Martin and I are very close.

As the weeks and months went by, I continued to press Ana for more information about my parents. I was concerned that recriminations would be taken against them because of my defection.

During the entire time of living in New York, I never received a letter from my parents. I found this to be very strange, especially since my father had found secretive ways to send letters from my mother to Ana in Israel years ago.

Ana, however, always deflected my concerns and seemed to avoid the subject at all costs. She continued to insist that I should not attempt to reach them directly.

"Eventually, Moishe, we may be able to place a call," she said. "But as long as our country is controlled by the Communists, it can't be done. They have agents that listen in on phone calls to your house, especially now that you have defected. If your parents are caught speaking to you, they could be interrogated and arrested. They could be charged with assisting your escape. In the meantime, you must be patient and continue to study hard, improve your English, and prepare to go to college. That's what Mother and your father would want you to do."

I listened, but there were many days when my mind wandered to Bratislava.

What is happening there?

Are my parents under suspicion?

Or worse, are they in danger?

Something just didn't seem right to me.

Nearly one year later, Ana approached me one morning as I entered the kitchen for breakfast.

"Moishe," she said. "I have some very sad news."

I braced myself, expecting the worst.

"I received a message from Aunt Helena. Your father has passed away."

I sat down at the table and stared straight ahead.

I was stunned.

She put her hand on my shoulder.

"I'm so sorry," she said.

After a few seconds, I gathered myself and looked up at her.

"Died? From what?" I asked.

"Kidney failure."

I winced and shook my head.

"Kidney failure? … I don't believe it. My father never had kidney disease. In fact, he never had any health issues. Are you sure?"

She paused for a few seconds.

She had an odd look on her face, apparently at loss for a response.

Her eyes darted nervously away from me, then toward the coffee pot as she reached over and began to pour a cup of coffee.

"That's all I know," she said coldly. "Aunt Helena offered no more details."

I became incensed.

"Ana … this is bullshit! You know it! I want the truth!

My father wouldn't have suddenly died from some kidney disease that he never had."

She immediately shut me down.

"I'm very sorry, Daniel. I know this is hard to accept. Losing a parent unexpectedly is a shock. But I have nothing more to say other than what I've already told you."

She seemed upset.

Her eyes welled up.

"I really can't talk about this anymore," she said as she quickly walked out of the kitchen.

I was numb.

My father had died, and I did not have the benefit of knowing all of the circumstances.

Had he been hospitalized for a long time? Or was his passing totally unexpected?

I had also been denied the usual outlets for mourning—no services at the temple, no funeral, no burial gathering, no chance to grieve alongside my mother.

A strange feeling of emptiness came over me.

I knew there had to be more to the story of my father's death.

Chapter Twenty-Two

IN 1967 I graduated from high school and enrolled at Long Island University. I was on track to receive my bachelor's degree in the Spring of 1971.

In March of 1970, I received some exciting news. My mother had negotiated a deal with the Slovakian-Communist Party in Bratislava to leave the country and emigrate to the United States.

This type of deal was no small feat, in itself. It required knowledge of the system, a broad base of "connections", skill in negotiating strategy, secrecy, and, of course, a lot of money. My mother always understood how to handle these corrupt local politicians—buying them off with cash was her usual opening offer.

Once again, this tactic worked to perfection.

She made a "donation" that helped her to gain the opportunity to present her case to the city's Governing Board. The seven local members were sympathetic to the plea of this sixty-five-year-old grandmother to be reunited with her daughter's family in New York. Of course, she made no mention of my presence in the United States and continued to deny any knowledge of my whereabouts.

The members of the Board listened and, in particular, were most appreciative of the additional generous sum she offered to the members as an "exit tax."

After a few minutes of private deliberation, they invited her back to the room to hear their counter-offer.

Not surprisingly, the greedy members of the Board recognized their own opportunity in this request and wanted a larger payoff.

In the end, her appeal was granted, provided that she would turn over the following: her house and all its contents, all funds in bank accounts, her entire pension, and all possessions, including cars, clothing, furs, jewelry, etc.

The only exception: she would be allowed to take one small suitcase filled with clothes and personal sundry items for her trip to the United States.

My mother understood that the opportunity to be reunited with her family, combined with the value of her freedom far exceeded the material value of her possessions.

She accepted the terms of this deal.

The members of the Governing Board were very pleased with this windfall of cash and the assets that had fallen into their laps.

However, they had totally underestimated my mother.

What they didn't know was that my mother had outsmarted them by secretly selling her house and all of its contents to her sister, Helena, weeks before the meeting. The Governing Board did not discover this information until my mother had already left the country.

They made a weak attempt to nullify the sale, but it had been certified and filed by an attorney who happened to be my mother's brother-in-law. Even in the corrupt city of Bratislava, further challenges to overturn the sale would have required a prolonged court proceeding, the details of which would have leaked out to the public. The members of the Governing Board would have been at risk—exposed as officials that had accepted bribes in exchange for government favors.

Such charges would have alerted the Russian overseers.

The repercussions to the members of the Board would have been serious—possibly resulting in criminal prosecution and imprisonment. Even worse, they might simply "disappear" and never be seen again.

Without any fanfare, they dropped the case.

Chapter Twenty-Three

MY MOTHER ARRIVED in New York on March 20, 1970.

Earlier that year, in a ceremony held in downtown Manhattan, Ana and I had become citizens of the United States. That day was so special because we had shared this memorable event together. It was, without doubt, one of the happiest days of our lives.

Our reunion with our mother at JFK Airport, however, was an even more emotional and joyous occasion. When she stepped from the Jetway and entered the terminal, the four of us—Ana, Oscar, Martin and I—let out a boisterous cheer.

My mother practically ran to us—excitedly shuffling her feet forward, with outstretched arms and a scream of pure joy—not knowing which one of the four of us she wanted to hug first.

I had never seen her so happy. And the reason was perfectly clear: My mother, Ana and I were in the United States! And, perhaps more importantly, for the first time in our lives, we were together in a place where we were all free!

My mother moved into Ana's house but soon recognized that the house was too small for five people. Eventually, my mother and I found a two-bedroom apartment in Flushing, NY.

My mother had been a seamstress during her younger years before the Nazis and Russians took over Czechoslovakia. Within months of her arrival in the United States, she rekindled her expertise in tailoring and established a highly successful women's clothing alteration business right out of our apartment. Considering the fact that she didn't know one word of English when she stepped off the airplane, her success was truly remarkable.

Over a period of only six months, by watching television and communicating with her customers, she improved her command of English, expanded her business and hired an employee.

My mother always amazed me.

She had arrived in this country without a penny to her name. Yet she had the ability to be creative—to deal with stressful situations and then adapt to survive.

When I look back on her life, the strength of her spirit and her determination to overcome all obstacles were extraordinary attributes that made her such a special person as well as a role model for her entire family.

One day, during our early months in the apartment, I took the opportunity to find closure with the details of my father's passing.

"Mother," I said. "Ana said Dad passed away from kidney failure. I never knew he had kidney problems. Is that true?"

My question surprised her.

She shook her head.

"I really don't want to talk about it," she said.

"Why? I need to know."

"It's a painful subject."

"How is it painful? He was my father; I have to know what happened to him."

Silence.

She seemed to be searching for the right way to begin or perhaps the best way to change the subject.

Finally, she spoke.

"After your escape, two officers came to our front door, early in the morning. They pounded so loudly, they frightened us nearly to death. I opened the door. They nearly knocked me to the floor as they burst in. They made your father and me sit on the couch. One of the officers took out his gun and pointed it at us...

the other searched the entire house, especially your room."

"Were they KGB?"

"KGB? No, they said they were the two officers who were guarding you when you escaped in Athens."

Chapter Twenty-Four

MY MOTHER'S WORDS shocked me.

In my wildest thoughts, I never imagined that those two guards would return to Bratislava and barge into my parents' house to get information on my whereabouts.

But it made perfect sense.

My escape had made them vulnerable to serious retribution and penalties from the KGB.

Possibly death.

If they could present information that would lead to my capture, perhaps their superiors and the KGB would go easier on them?

"What did they say to you?" I asked my mother.

"The tall one seemed to be in charge. He demanded to know where you were. Who was hiding you? Did we know you were going to escape? Did we help you to plan it?"

"Did they threaten you?"

"Threaten?" she asked sarcastically. "They did more than threaten; they terrorized us. The shorter, fat one said nothing when he got done searching the house. He just stood there pointing his gun at us while the one in charge kept yelling questions into our faces. We tried to explain that we had no information and didn't even know you had escaped."

Her voice got louder and cracked with emotion and anger.

Tears rolled down her face.

"Then they put us into separate rooms and continued interrogating us for more than another hour. The fat guard took me into the kitchen and kept up with the same questions. What did I know? How did I help you? Did I plan your escape? Did I know where you were? Have I been in contact with you?"

She stopped, sat down and wiped her eyes with a towel from the kitchen table.

Then she looked up, as if struck by a revelation.

"But he looked nervous and was sweating profusely. I actually asked him why he seemed so desperate ... so afraid. He said his life depended on capturing you and bringing you back to Bratislava."

She paused again, took a deep breath and exhaled in resignation.

"Then they brought us back to the family room and made us sit side by side on the couch. The taller one took out his gun and threatened to shoot your father right in front of me if I didn't talk. I begged him to stop and kept pleading for him to understand that we had nothing to offer."

I fumbled for the right words.

"I'm sorry I did that to you," I said.

It was admittedly a weak apology, but all I could come up with.

My mother was quick to respond.

Her eyes narrowed and she became adamant.

"No! Don't be sorry…never…not even for one minute!" she said as her voice rose loudly. "We were proud of what you did…that you had the strength and determination to somehow get away from those monsters. To this day, I don't know the details of your escape. I don't need to know! All that matters is that you are a free man…don't ever let anyone take that away from you!"

She looked away.

She said nothing, but nodded as if recalling the images of that traumatic day.

Then she looked up at me.

"I never wanted you to know all of this. I didn't want you to feel guilty…thinking that you were responsible for what happened to us. You did what had to be done. You would have had no life in a country run by those terrible people. I was so proud of you when Helena brought Ana's message to me ... 'the goods have arrived in New York'. The sweetest words I ever heard. How I cried that day ... but they were tears of joy."

She stood up and hugged me.

It was a special moment.

Unforgettable.

I remember it to this day.

But I still had questions.

I leaned back.

I looked into her eyes.

"Did the Russians leave you alone after that?"

She looked down and shook her head.

Her face saddened.

"No, the KGB came to the house two days later."

Chapter Twenty-Five

I PRESSED ON for more details.

"What did the KGB want? Didn't the two guards tell them you had nothing to offer?"

She smirked.

"The KGB? They were all business. Two senior officers and four younger ones. One of the senior officers forced us to sit on our couch while he stood over us, shouted orders and asked us the same questions we had answered for the two Slovakian guards. Then he directed the younger ones to go to your room. They opened the closets and emptied all the drawers onto the floor. They took everything that belonged to you… your clothes, your shoes, your pictures, the toys from your younger years, your tennis racquets…every possible tangible memory we had of you. Then they threw them into large boxes and bags and took them to a truck that was parked outside."

I was stunned.

"Why? Why would they want those things?" I asked.

"Because they wanted to destroy every morsel of your being...as if you never existed ... to deny us any pleasure in remembering you."

I was speechless.

She reached for the small towel, wiped her eyes again and sat down at the table.

I knew she had more to tell me.

But she seemed to be holding back.

I tried to gently push for answers.

"Did they continue to interrogate you?"

She paused for a few seconds and then answered in a near whisper.

"Yes, they were brutal. But we knew nothing. We had no information to give them."

"So ... did they just leave?"

"No. They became angry and accused us of hiding the truth and not cooperating. We kept trying to explain that we didn't know where you were or whether you were even still alive."

She stopped and tried to gather herself. Re-telling this story had taken an emotional toll on her.

But she collected herself and continued.

"Then the senior KGB officer leaned over to me and asked if I knew what they did to discourage defectors and those who assist them. I simply shook my head and said 'No.' Then he stood up proudly to say that the two guards that came to our house two days ago had been executed by firing squad."

She put her head down and shook it from side to side while beginning to sob.

I stepped closer and placed my hand on her shoulder.

Although I had long suspected that this would be the deadly fate for the two guards, hearing it being confirmed by my mother was most disconcerting.

I felt a sudden pit in my stomach as my mind raced back to images of them sitting with me at the table in the Athena Restaurant. The harsh reality that my escape had directly led to the death of these two individuals shook me to my core.

But my mother continued, and her riveting words quickly brought me back to the present time.

"I understood what he meant," she said slowly, "and what he was threatening to do. I told him again that we knew nothing. But he didn't believe me. Then he turned to the younger officers and gave a signal. Two of them moved closer to your father ...one stood in front of him and held him by his shoulders while the other grabbed his arms, pulled them behind his back, and put him into handcuffs."

She stopped for a moment to gather herself once again.

The recounting of this story had brought back excruciating memories.

She took a deep breath before she was able to continue.

"Then they took your father away," she said in a voice halting with more emotion. "He turned to look back to me just as they were putting him into their car. When our eyes met, we both knew we would never see each other again."

"They put him in prison?"

She looked down again.

This time she paused for a longer time.

I could tell that she was torn by what she was about to say.

Then she looked straight into my eyes.

"No, Daniel. Your father was poisoned."

My heart sank.

I sat down next to her, trying to process everything that she had just unburdened.

I reached out and held her hand.

No words were spoken.

We wept quietly.

After a short while, she slowly nodded a few times—in a manner of final acceptance.

Then she looked off—away from me—as if talking to someone else.

"After all," she said. "That is the Russian way."

Chapter Twenty-Six

OVER THE COURSE of the next fifteen years, my life underwent many changes which can only be described as "some ups and some downs."

I graduated from college and landed a job as an assistant tennis professional. I stayed on in that position for a year and a half and, eventually, was offered the position of Head Tennis Professional at the Forest Park Tennis and Racquet Club.

I got married and our first child—a son—was born in 1977.

My reputation as a tennis professional grew in the Long Island area, and I was offered a position in Massapequa where I was in charge of three tennis facilities. I remained in that job for six years. However, the mid-1980s experienced a decline in interest in tennis clubs. Memberships dropped off considerably.

I began to look into the possibilities of a new career.

A neighbor, Bob, had experience as a distributor of frozen seafood and was seeking a partner to establish a new business. This was a totally new venture for me, but the possibilities were intriguing.

I joined him in forming a partnership.

For a while our new company prospered. However, I discovered several discrepancies during a bookkeeping audit. When I confronted my partner, it became apparent that he had been skimming money off our profits to support his cocaine addiction.

We dissolved the partnership.

I moved on to other business ventures within the food industry. I achieved great success with a company that prepared beef, chicken and seafood for home delivery.

During this same time, my first marriage, that had produced two wonderful sons, encountered some difficult times and ended up in divorce.

Fortunately, I met my present wife, Karina, at Crest Hollow Country Club on Long Island where I was employed as a part-time tennis instructor. We have been happily married for more than thirty-seven years.

Ana and Oscar retired and moved to Fort Lauderdale, Florida in the late 1980s. My mother, ever full of energy and possessing a strong work ethic, continued her clothing alteration business into her eighties.

In 1990, however, she was diagnosed with pancreatic cancer.

Her treatments and after-care required considerable support, so she moved to Florida to live with Ana until her final days.

My mother, Erna "Netty" Kolmann passed away in 1991.

She was 86 years old.

Chapter Twenty-Seven

IN 1989, THE people of Czechoslovakia, following the lead of other countries in the Soviet Bloc, revolted against Russian dominance by means of a nonviolent transition of power known as The Velvet Revolution. During November and December of 1989, popular demonstrations were held in which protesters, including students and other dissidents, railed against the one-party government of the Communist Party of Czechoslovakia (CCP). With no support from a seriously weakened Russia, the CCP crumbled, bringing about the end of forty-one years of one-party rule in Czechoslovakia. This resulted in a dismantling of the command economy—where the government controls production, distribution and pricing—and the conversion to a parliamentary republic. (5)

In June 1990, Czechoslovakia held its first democratic elections since 1946.

In January 1993, Czechoslovakia split into two independent, democratic countries—the Czech Republic and Slovakia.

Fortunately, my mother had lived just long enough to enjoy the news of most of these revolutionary changes in her home country.

In 2007, my wife encouraged me to return to Bratislava—my home city. For several years, my Aunt Helena and her other sister, Olga, had invited us to visit them and see all of the positive changes that had occurred since the end of Russian and Communist control of the city.

Aunt Olga's son, Karl had a very successful business in Bratislava, similar to the American version of Home Depot. He offered to be our guide if we decided to visit the city.

In addition, my aging Aunt Helena had secretly stored my mother's possessions from her home and wanted me to sort through these items and ship any that were of value back to the United States while she was still alive.

My aunt had also sold my mother's house to an elderly couple with whom she was on very good terms. She said she could arrange for me to visit the home where I had grown up.

Before my mother passed away, she shared a very interesting story with me. She had a collection of solid gold coins that she could not hide in the small suitcase that she was allowed to take out of the country.

She was also determined to not let the corrupt Communist members of the Government Board get their hands on these coins. Aunt Helena had refused to hide them in her house. If the coins had been discovered during a routine search by the Communist authorities, the penalties to the homeowner would have been severe, including long-term imprisonment.

In one of her final acts of defiance, my mother had buried a box with the gold coins—wrapped safely inside—under a tree in the backyard of our house. Of course, she had no idea whether the box was still there or if it might have been uncovered or destroyed during landscaping or construction.

Nevertheless, she wanted me to know of its existence in case I had the opportunity to recover her "hidden treasure."

Despite Karina's urgings, I had misgivings about returning to Bratislava.

Slovakia was now a free country, but media reports continued to describe the rampant corruption of government officials.

Would crossing the border into Slovakia trigger a report that I had defected?

Would government officials take some action against me?

In the end, I considered a visit to my aunt and my

cousin as a family obligation, as well as an opportunity to bring some level of closure to the traumatic experience of my defection.

Karina and I flew to Vienna and rented a car to drive to Bratislava. As we got closer to the border of Slovakia, I began to feel uneasy.

Perhaps paranoid is a better description.

I pulled the car to the side of the road and stopped.

"What's wrong?" asked Karina.

"I'm not sure about this," I said.

"Not sure? Why? You're an American citizen. You've done nothing wrong."

"But the country still has Communist sympathizers—Slovakians who joined the Russian Army to save their own necks and turned against their own neighbors. People like me who defected exposed them for the atrocities they committed against Slovakian citizens. They may hold a grudge."

Karina understood my feelings.

"Let me drive so you can try to relax," she said.

We switched seats and Karina drove the car the rest of the way to the border gates between Austria and Slovakia.

We passed through the gate exiting Austria without delay. The line of cars, however, waiting to be processed to enter Slovakia was ten deep. We waited nearly half an hour before pulling up to the guard booth that was manned by a border guard that appeared to be in his mid-30s.

"Passports," he said with a scowl.

"Good morning," Karina said as she handed our passports to him.

He ignored her greeting.

The guard looked over the passports and scanned the information into a computer.

He stared at the computer screen for a few seconds and then back at our passports.

This back-and-forth process repeated itself several times.

He seemed troubled by the information on his computer screen.

Something's wrong, I thought.

Karina flashed a look toward me, then quickly averted my eyes before I could say anything.

Her signal was clear: *This is no time for conversation.*

A long, agonizing minute passed.

The guard leaned over to our car and directed his words to me.

"Sir," he said in Slovakian. "There's a citizen of Bratislava with the same name and birth date."

I cringed.

"Yes, that's me," I said with a forced smile. "I left

when I was sixteen and never came back. I stayed in the United States and lived with my sister."

He looked at my passport for a third time and then, once again, at his computer screen.

We waited.

Another agonizing moment.

He leaned out of his booth and pointed to a small parking area to the right. "Back up and pull your car over there, please, and wait until I check a few things."

Karina complied with his request and parked the car.

Twenty minutes passed.

A nerve-wracking eternity.

Finally, he walked out of the booth and handed Karina's passport to her. He leaned into the driver-side window and stared over at me for a few seconds without saying a word. Then he glanced down at my passport for another look at my picture.

"Why is there no record that you left the country?" he asked.

"I have no idea," I said.

He flashed a sarcastic half-smile.

I said nothing.

"So, you're just returning to visit your Mother Land?"

"Yes," I said.

He stared at me for a few more seconds, then turned

and walked back to his booth. Finally, as he stood in front of the computer, he shrugged and stamped my passport. Then he walked over to our car and handed it back to Karina.

Back in the booth, he pressed a button to open the gate.

"Have a nice day," he said in English as we drove through.

I looked at Karina and breathed a sigh of relief.

This brief encounter confirmed that I was still "on the books" in Slovakia.

My birth had been recorded, but not the date that I had gone missing.

Technically, I had never left the country, and they had simply lost track of me for forty-three years.

We arrived in Bratislava within forty minutes.

Our first stop was the area of the Sports Camp where I was taken as a twelve-year old. Although much of the property had undergone new construction and land-scaping changes in the forty-three years since I left it, vestiges of the original facility remained.

The five-story dormitory building that housed the athletes remained in its pristine location on top of the hill overlooking the Danube River.

New tennis courts and a brand-new soccer field and practice facility had replaced those that I remembered.

However, a cement wall near the tennis courts remained intact. This was the same wall I used as a backboard to practice my ground strokes in tennis. During my four years at the Sports Camp, I must have hit tens of thousands of tennis balls against this wall.

I walked over to the wall.

I recalled the hours—especially those during my final year at the camp, when I stood alone in that spot hitting tennis balls against this wall, all the while contemplating my future.

How could I escape?

Would I be caught?

Then tortured and killed?

Or would I be free?

Did I have the courage to try?

It was an emotional moment.

Karina walked over to me.

She saw the strained look on my face.

She seemed puzzled.

"Are you okay? You've been standing next to this wall for a long time."

I stood silently.

Karina took my arm. "Does this wall have some special meaning for you? Did something happen here?" she asked.

CHAPTER TWENTY-SEVEN

Her questions snapped me back to reality.

I smiled.

"This is the place where I finally decided to be a man."

Chapter Twenty-Eight

WE LEFT THE Sports Camp and continued the drive into the center of Bratislava.

I was surprised at myself for remembering the streets and the directions to get to my old house.

But nothing much had changed.

We drove right there.

My cousin, Karl, had received my call and was waiting for us.

An older woman stood next to him.

But it wasn't my Aunt Helena.

I got out of the car and looked all around.

The same uneasy feeling came over me for the second time.

Karl hugged me immediately.

"Daniel!" he said. "Welcome home! It's been so many years."

"Yes, I wasn't sure if I'd ever come back here. Thank you for meeting us."

I introduced Karina to Karl and then looked at the

older woman who had stood smiling at me but had never said a word.

She pointed to a nearby house and began to speak.

"I'm Dr. Freid. You probably don't remember me but I have lived in that house for nearly forty-five years. I knew your parents and remember you very well."

I shook her hand and smiled, but I had no recollection of her.

It was an awkward moment.

Karl bailed me out.

"Are you ready to go inside and see your old house? I told the owners you'd be coming over today. He's a disabled veteran ... served in the Russian military for a long time."

I swallowed hard.

"Russian military?" I asked.

"Yes. He's Slovakian but joined the military while the Russians were in control."

He grabbed me by the arm and started to lead me toward the front door.

I stopped.

"Karl, I'll be more comfortable if you knock on the door first and make sure they don't mind meeting me."

"Are you sure?"

"Yes, I'll just wait in the car until you give me a signal."

Karl looked a bit perplexed.

Karina sensed his confusion.

"I'll go with you, Karl. Daniel will walk a little way behind us until we're sure they won't mind our visit."

She gave me a look.

I got her message.

Karl and Karina walked up to the door as I waited on the sidewalk, a short distance away from them, still somewhat unsure about this entire idea.

Former Russian military? Does this man know my history?

Karl rang the doorbell.

The door opened and an old woman stood in the doorway.

She had long, gray stringy hair.

Her clothes were dirty and disheveled.

She listened to what Karl was saying and then peered over his shoulder to catch a glimpse of me standing on the sidewalk.

Then she turned and called for her husband to come to the door.

"Peter!" she yelled. "They're here!"

She turned back and looked at Karina.

"What's with him?" as she gestured toward me. "He's not coming in?"

Karina blushed.

"No, he's just waiting to make sure it's all right with your husband."

A tapping sound began to come from the house.

The noise gradually increased in intensity to become a rhythmical pounding.

One two, one two, one two.

Over and over.

A short man finally appeared in the doorway. He had a very unusual limp which required a rope attached to the underside of one of his shoes—one with a large leather heel to compensate for a noticeably shorter leg. After one step forward with his good foot, he pulled the rope upward in order to drag the other foot forward and take a step.

"This is my husband, Peter," the old woman said. "He was wounded in the war, but he still manages to get around."

"Yes, I see," said Karina. "Thank you for letting us come by. My husband was born and raised in this house."

"Yes, we heard that," she said.

Then she turned and waved me in from the sidewalk.

"If you want to see your old house, you won't be able to see much from out there," she said.

I couldn't delay much longer.

I walked up and stood next to Karina.

CHAPTER TWENTY-EIGHT

The old couple stepped aside as we walked in through the doorway.

Peter said nothing.

He just looked me over.

For some reason, I was filled with anxiety.

But a major distraction caused me to get over my apprehension as soon as we entered—the house was filthy and rundown.

A disgusting, musty odor pervaded the entire interior.

It was obvious that these two elderly people did not have the ability or the wherewithal to care for this house.

I walked into my bedroom.

Other than my bed and dresser—the same ones I used years ago when I was a child—the room was stark and bare. I resisted the urge to open a few of the drawers to see if any of my things were still there.

Perhaps the Russians had missed something when they rummaged through my belongings?

The very thought of doing so made me laugh.

I didn't touch anything.

The paint on the walls had faded and, in some areas, had begun to peel. Obviously, the room had not been painted since I left forty-three years ago.

I was struck by an odd feeling—the house appeared so much smaller than I remembered.

I honestly felt that way, but doesn't everyone who visits their childhood home?

I walked out to the living room—the area where my father had built a "fake wall" so my mother could hide non-perishable items during the frequent periods of extreme food shortages.

The wall was still there, but I decided not to ask the elderly couple if they had ever discovered what was behind it. Besides, my mother must have removed whatever currency had been hidden there before she left Bratislava for the United States.

We walked outside to the back yard.

The elderly couple followed me without saying a word.

The electrified fence and the concrete bunker were still there.

Memories of my father flashed through my mind.

There were six trees in the rear of the property. I couldn't remember how many were there when I lived in the house. But these trees were much larger. I thought of my mother's gold coins—hidden in a box under one of those trees.

But which one?

After all this time, someone could dig for days and never find them.

Or had they been found already?

These two old people certainly didn't look like they had found a small fortune in gold.

Besides, if I found the gold coins on their property, how could I claim ownership? More importantly, how could I get the gold coins out of the country without risking legal entanglement?

I decided not to even mention the subject.

There are times in life when you just have to let go of some things.

For me, this was one of those times.

The brief tour of my old house ended fairly quickly. Despite my earlier apprehension, I had reached a moment of calm and acceptance.

The city of Bratislava and my house had formed my roots—the place where my life began. Seeing them again reinforced the value and importance of my journey to get away from them.

I paused for a few seconds for one final look.

I knew I would never see this house again.

Karina took my hand. "Seen enough?" she asked.

I sighed.

"Yes. Let's go," I said.

We thanked the old couple and walked to the front door.

Karl had already left to wait by the car.

Or, at least that's what I had been led to believe.

We came out of the house and were greeted by a thunderous cheer.

I was shocked by the scene before us.

More than seventy-five people—neighbors and friends of the doctor who remembered me—had gathered outside of the house. Some were older; others my age; many were teenagers or younger children.

They clapped their hands and called my name.

"Daniel! Daniel! Daniel!" they yelled.

It was a wild scene.

Then, one by one, they came over and formed a line to shake my hand and congratulate me. The teenage girls were giddy. A few asked for my autograph.

I was completely taken aback by this outpouring of affection.

I looked over to Dr. Freid. "What's happening? Why have all these people come here?"

She smiled.

"Because you are a hero," she said.

I shook my head.

"Me? A hero? I don't understand."

"You did what so many of them wanted to do, but never were brave enough or had the opportunity. You escaped and got away from the Communist oppressors. People talked about you for years. They told their children. You were an inspiration for them. When Karl told me you were coming today, I spread the word around the neighborhood. They just had to meet you."

I turned to Karl. "You knew about this?"

He laughed. "When the doctor told me her plan, I thought it might make a nice surprise. You never knew it, Daniel ... you were only sixteen, but you made a lot of people in this city very proud."

I stepped back and looked over the long line of people still waiting to greet me. I immediately thought of my mother's reaction when she heard the words, "The goods have arrived in New York."

On that day, she had cried tears of joy.

Well, forty-three years later, the "goods" had come full circle and had returned to Bratislava.

And, of course, tears of joy began to run down my cheeks.

Epilogue

MY LIFE IN the United States can only be described as one filled with gratitude, love and happiness. Throughout my adult years I have been able to find success, not only on the tennis court as a teaching professional, but in the business world.

More importantly, I am blessed to have a wonderful wife, Karina, two grown children and nine grandchildren.

Sadly, my half-sister, Ana Berman, passed away in October 2010. Like our mother, Ana had a remarkable and positive influence on my life. I will always be indebted to her for her love, advice, guidance, and inspiration to escape from the terrors of Russian-occupied Czechoslovakia. Her son—my nephew, Martin—remains as a close part of my extended family.

My story—like so many other stories of people who escaped from political oppression and tyranny—is an example of the power of the human spirit to risk everything to find freedom.

May it inspire others to do the same.

References

1. Prague in Black: Nazi Rule and Czech Nationalism. Chad Bryant, Harvard University Press, September, 2009.

2. totallyhistory.com/german-occupation-of-Czecho-slovakia

3. encyclopedia.ushmm.org/content/en/article/ the_holocaust_in_bohemia_and_moravia

4. Communist Czechoslovakia 1945-1989. Kevin McDermott, Red Globe Press, August 2015.

5. The Velvet Revolution: 30 Years After. Monika MacDonagh-Pajerova, et al, Karolinum Press, Charles University, January, 2020.

A Few Words from the Author

THROUGHOUT THE TEXT of this book, the name of the main character is listed as Daniel Kolmann. This name is a pseudonym since the family of this man has requested that he remain anonymous for fear that he, or other members of his family, could be the target of antisemitic repercussions. Nevertheless, all aspects of his story are true and I greatly appreciate that he sought me out to write the compelling story of his defection from Communist-occupied Czechoslovakia during the post-World War II era. May his daring escape from tyranny and totalitarianism serve as an inspiration to others who value freedom.

The author also thanks the following people who made valuable contributions to the writing of this book:

My preview readers: Kristen Rzezuski, Phyllis Oblas, Nadia Frye, Alan Fine, Joe Bellargo, and Robin Boretti. Thank you for the hours you spent reading the early drafts and providing thoughtful comments and encouragement that helped bring the final manuscript to fruition.

Ronney O'Donnell for her expert, painstaking editing of the manuscript. Whenever I was in doubt, she always came up with the right word.

Joseph P. O'Donnell

About the Author

Joseph P. O'Donnell is the author of the Gallagher Trilogy of Mystery Thrillers: **Fatal Gamble**, **Deadly Codes** and **Pulse of My Heart**. The feature-length motion picture **Bent (2018)** is based on characters he created in the Gallagher novels. In 2022, O'Donnell published **Living on the Fringe of the Mob**, a memoir about a man who was connected to the New York Mob for his entire life. This book is currently being formatted into a nine-episode miniseries.

Run for My Life is his second book in the genre of memoir.

9 781977 260086